GOOD NEWS, GREAT JOY
AN ADVENT DEVOTIONAL

AN ADVENT DEVOTIONAL

by Graham Jones

Good News, Great Joy: An Advent Devotional

Copyright © 2021 by Graham Jones

Independently Published

Art by Grace Cook

First printed 2021, Second Edition published 2022

Printed in the United States of America

All emphases in Scripture quotations have been added by the author.

ISBN: 978-0-578-98947-1

For Luke, my son

Contents

— Introduction —

Several years ago, as Advent approached, I was longing for a way to get at the heart of its story. After studying the Gospel of Luke, I was intrigued by its telling of Christ's birth. Compared to the regular depictions of the nativity of Christ, Luke contains a strange yet rich account of how a promised king makes an unexpectedly humble arrival. This king from Bethlehem has become the source of hope and object of worship for some two billion people all over the planet.

As one from that multitude, I came to saving faith in Jesus at a young age, and God has been kind to help me grow in my faith in the years since. I love Christmas, as my close friends and family can attest, but I want to love its Christ even more.

That desire is what drove me to get at the heart of the Christmas story years ago. Some people seem satisfied with enjoying the surface level meaning, like skimming through their favorite scenes from their favorite movie, but I wanted to dig deep into the details of the story of Jesus's birth—the extended edition, behind-the-scenes account of things.

Songwriting is one way that I process deep things in life and in Scripture, so with my dear friend Preston, I went to work trying to unpack the meaning in these biblical passages.

Thankfully, this kind of story investigation was exactly Luke's purpose in writing. If you read the opening four verses of Luke, you know that he wrote with the express purpose of building certainty in a man named Theophilus regarding Jesus—the mysterious king whose life, death, and resurrection started a vast, global movement.

Through our study and songwriting, we began to put together a project to share with our local church. We called it Good News, Great Joy, so named because of the declaration of the angel to the shepherds in Luke 2:10. We sought to highlight the announcement of God's salvation in the coming of Christ and the responses of those first hearers. How was this news good and why did it bring them great joy?

What began as a four-song suite based on a few passages slowly transformed over many years into an eleven-song album which covers all of Luke 1:5-2:20 in detail. We have performed these songs for our church family on Christmas Eve every year since. In 2020, by God's kindness and the generosity of many, I was able to fund the recording and production of this album. As a part of that fundraiser, it only seemed fitting to offer to write a few devotionals as a thank-you gift to those who had given and as a way to honor the origin of this music. These twenty-five readings walk through the songs of the album in coordination with the passages that inspired them.

Disclaimer: I am not a Bible scholar nor a proficient writer. All the same, I hope that God will take these meager efforts and multiply them, as he has done for me in my heart through these months of studying and writing.

Use this book as a tool to engage with God's word during the season of Advent. Read the devotionals alone in the morning before work, out at lunch with a friend, or together with your family at night. Take the time to read the daily passages from God's word suggested at the top before diving into the devotional itself. Consider how you can apply the truths you read. Conclude your time in prayer and ask for God's Spirit to transform you.

However you use them, I offer these Advent devotionals to you in the same hope Luke held for his friend Theophilus: that you will draw near to Christ and discover the same certainty of faith in him. I hope that you will hear about his loving work to save you through his death on the cross and resurrection from the grave, put your faith in him, and be strengthened and equipped to walk by faith in him day after day.

The good news of Jesus brought great joy to its hearers back then. May it do the same for us this Advent as we journey through the story of its unfolding together.

The Coming King

Who is he? Is he not the king?
Prophesied of old
Coming for his people

MICAH 4:6-5:5

Thanksgiving is over. Fall decorations have been boxed away, making way for twice as many boxes of garland and lights and trinkets and ornaments. The consumer world has long since adjusted its marketing and music for the season. TV channels and streaming services offer thousands of hours of holiday specials, new and old. Choirs sing, orchestras play, friends party, families gather. "Christmastime is here," goes the song, and so goes the world.

At least, this is our world, for those of us living in America and in similar cultures around the globe. Though fraught with the real dangers of excess and misuse, the Christmas season is a wonderful time filled with rich memories, great wonder, and nostalgic melancholy that leads to joy.

But why all of the seasonal focus and fuss? Why all of the immense expectation and meaning?

Those of us who follow Jesus often try to answer that question with Advent liturgies, holiday traditions, and stitched pillows reading, "Jesus is the Reason for the Season!" while spending the days running back and forth to parties, plans, performances, and all kinds of other seasonal pleasures that, if we're honest, don't bring us an inch closer to the real Jesus.

Long before the real Jesus ever showed up on the scene, there was a people called Israel who had been promised an eternal king. God had made himself known by calling and saving this people who routinely found themselves cast out and oppressed by rulers across the ages. Their ancestors were sent to a foreign land and endured unjust hardship, even to the point of being made into slaves in Egypt. Their ancient tribes were oppressed under Pharaoh and attacked by surrounding nations on the journey to their land of promise. Even in this land, their nation faced repeated oppression, occupation, slavery, and exile that faithful prophets would warn against but no hero or king could permanently fix. From sinful consequence to suffering circumstance, this cycle continued in perpetuity through the ages. Where was the promised King?

Our world runs this same course year after year. There is no kingdom, regardless of government, prosperity, or cultural accomplishment, where people are not oppressed and tyrants do not hold sway. There is no nation where sin and suffering do not abide. Within our own lives, our personal kingdoms are fraught with the same cyclical problems, whether we recognize them or not.

How often do we attempt to wrap our hope in the trappings of this season? With good intention, we long for the extra money spent on gifts and experiences to give us great joy, for the extra time spent on events and plans to give us purpose, for the extra effort spent on going to church, giving to charity, and engaging in culture wars to give us meaning. When those things rule us, we're just one panic attack, unexpected bill, trauma, or family drama away from falling down even further into the despair from which we first tried to escape.

In the midst of our dark world, we, like the people Israel, need an eternal king.

This king was the hope of the prophets, through whom the Lord spoke to his people. Matthew's gospel speaks of Magi in the first century, perhaps pagan Persian priests who were well-acquainted with such prophecies because of Israel's time in exile in their land. Whatever their background, they had come to such a strong belief in God's promises that they were studying, waiting, and watching expectantly for his king to come out of Bethlehem.

The Magi knew where to look because they knew God's word, specifically in Micah 5:2: "But you, O Bethlehem Ephrathah, who are too little to be among the clans of Judah, from you shall come forth for me one who is to be ruler in Israel, whose coming forth is from of old, from ancient days." God spoke through the prophet Micah about Israel's coming destruction and exile. God asked them, "Now why do you cry aloud? Is there no king in you?"[1] and then proceeded to show them that while judgment would come for the wicked, peace would follow for the faithful. That promised peace would come through a forever king, a perfect ruler who would come from the small town of Bethlehem.

Advent is a time for our hearts and minds to be especially focused on the same Scriptures that so intrigued the Magi in the years prior to the coming of Jesus. Their posture should be ours, as well, so that we might draw closer to the truth and peace that God has promised in Christ. What better time than Advent to increase our time in God's word, to look once again with anticipation to the king of promise? The same king that was the focus of the Magi and prophesied in the Scriptures is also our hope today.

Let us set up our lights and nativities, go to parties and concerts, and celebrate this season with great excitement, but let us, even more so, press in to the real source of hope—for even now, we still anticipate the second coming of this king, and his kingdom is not one we might expect.

---

1   Micah 4:9

— Day 2 —

Good News
PART I

Chosen by the Lord, Zechariah came
Through the temple doors, as the people prayed

LUKE 1:5-17

Advent is a time for hope and longing. The songs we sing, the lights we hang, our evergreen Christmas trees…even the length of the holiday season reflects this.

As discussed in the previous devotional, this longing should point us to the coming of a savior king, but if we're honest with ourselves, we are often more satisfied with the trappings of hope than with its source. Would we still long for Jesus with the same fervor and passion without all these good things that fill this time of year? The Christmas season offers us countless temptations to become focused on stuff *about* Jesus outside of our hope *in* Jesus himself.

Luke begins the story of Jesus's coming with a seemingly random old priest, Zechariah, and his barren wife Elizabeth. Despite their lot in life, Luke wants us to know of their righteousness before the Lord. Neither of them were perfect (as Zechariah will soon prove), but they remained faithful to the Lord even though they lacked the object of their greatest longings: a child.

Zechariah and Elizabeth's barrenness echoes that of Abram and Sarai from the Old Testament. After years of waiting for God to make good on his promise to make Abram a father of many nations through his "very own son," Abram abandoned the hope of ever having a son with his wife Sarai. They took matters into their own hands, and Abram had a son with Sarai's servant, Hagar.[1]

Abram's story offers us a warning. How faithful are we to God when life doesn't quickly give us our hopes and desires? Even when they are for good and godly things, we can struggle to trust our good God to give them in his own timing, or to find our ultimate satisfaction in him. Instead, like Abram and Sarai, we often trust in our own strength and turn to our own ways.

Consider how Luke describes Zechariah and Elizabeth in contrast. Their barrenness and longing to have children did not hinder their faith and obedience to the Lord, but was, in fact, the setting for their flourishing faith.

We can assume by their age that most of their married life was spent waiting and longing for children. Through all this, they walked "blamelessly in all the commandments and statutes of the Lord."[2] If they were walking in obedience to the Lord only in an effort to gain what they hoped for, they would have abandoned their obedience years before, but Luke tells us that they were both "advanced in years."[3] The righteousness of Zechariah and Elizabeth did not stem from their circumstances or their obedience, but from their faith in the Lord.

Not by accident did the Lord send his message to this faithful priest at the altar of incense in the temple of Jerusalem. This altar was set up in front of the veil and the mercy seat, where the presence of God dwelt as he met with his people.[4] The offerings and sacrifices made in that holy place were a constant reminder of God's presence, of his covenant love and mercy toward his people. This is the altar where God met Zechariah with good news. Years later, the promised savior king would

---

1   Genesis 15:4, 16:1-16
2   Luke 1:6
3   Luke 1:7
4   Exodus 30

give his life on a cross and the veil in that temple would tear from top to bottom, announcing that God has come to give unfettered access to himself through faith in Jesus Christ.

Friend, the good news of Christmas is not that we can reach God through our own devices, but that the real presence of God in Christ came down to reach us. No matter what objects we hold most dear or what good things we long for, nothing can compete with the eternal presence of our Creator, offered freely through faith in our Savior, who fills us with his Spirit. The hope of Christianity is not rooted in things of any kind, but in God himself.

Maybe this season didn't start out like you hoped. Maybe you started day one of Advent with great intentions for godly rhythms and have already fallen behind. Maybe, for whatever reason, it just doesn't feel like Christmas this year. Whatever your circumstances, turn from trying to gain access to God by your works and circumstances, and simply come to him through faith in Jesus, the one who came down for you. His gospel—his promised birth, perfect life, death, and resurrection—is our greatest gift, given that we may live by faith in him, no matter what else we have.

Good News
Part II

For God has heard your prayers and he is sending you a child
For there is great joy in the plans of God

LUKE 1:8-25

If you think about it, Charles Dickens's *A Christmas Carol* is actually a pretty terrifying story. In it (spoiler alert), a man named Ebenezer Scrooge hates Christmas and loves money. He is visited by the ghost of his dead friend who warns him that he will spend eternity in heavy chains if he doesn't listen to three other ghosts coming to haunt him. It's only after seeing a vision of his death that he has a change of heart and decides to live more generously, with the spirit of Christmas suddenly alive and well in him.

One could summarize it this way: an old man must be haunted by ghosts and shown a vision of dying alone and unloved to be scared into living a generous life. Wow. Merry Christmas.

I'm being flippant, of course. I actually love the story of *A Christmas Carol*, but I think the darkness and strangeness of it is worth considering in light of Zechariah's story.

We may not all be Scrooges, but we are all by nature a skeptical people toward the truth. From the very beginning, our minds are haunted by that pressing question, "did God actually say…?"[1] Think about yourself for a moment. In what areas are you most skeptical? What does it take for you to be convinced of your own fallacy and submit to the truth?

---

1   Genesis 3:1

Consider what it took for Zechariah in Luke 1:5-25—a silent tongue and open ears.

Luke intentionally mirrors his wording from the opening few verses when he describes Zechariah's response to the angel's message. He hopes Theophilus will "have certainty" about the things he has been taught,[2] or better put, that he will *really know* the true word. When the angel Gabriel tells Zechariah how God will provide him a child in his old age, Zechariah responds with, "How will I *really know* this?" How often we have also questioned God's word!

Gabriel's response to this question is strange: "I am Gabriel." So what? Why does anyone care about his name? We may not understand the significance, but this old, faithful priest did. The angel who appeared to Zechariah also appeared hundreds of years prior to a prophet named Daniel. In that context, Daniel was earnestly praying for the people of Israel when an angel of the Lord appeared before him. He announced himself as Gabriel and said, "At the beginning of your pleas for mercy a word went out, and I have come to tell it to you, for you are greatly loved. Therefore consider the word and understand the vision."[3]

In Daniel's life and in Zechariah's, God sent Gabriel to prove that he hears the prayers of his people because he loves them. When God reveals his love for his people, he calls them to consider, understand, and obey his word. Daniel responded this way, but Zechariah doubts God's answer, even while an entire crowd of people are praying for him outside![4]

What about you? When you pray, do you pray as if God hears you? When you read God's word, do you consider what he has to say about your present circumstances? When you understand God's answer, do you trust him?

---

2   Luke 1:1-4
3   Daniel 9:23
4   Luke 1:10

Our attitude toward God's word reflects our trust in God's character, and our trust in God's character is reflected in our prayers. The God who speaks to us in his word is the same God who made us and saves us through faith in Jesus Christ. Though entirely impossible in our own strength, God has come down and brought life to us through him.

For all of us who have experienced this new life in Jesus, we should amplify the Scriptural testimonies of his life, death, and resurrection. During this season, the testimony of God's miraculous incarnation should fill us with wonder. As we encounter his word in our daily lives, we ought to consider: will we also respond with faith and trust? Will we display that trust in him by seeking to understand and obey him more and more?

Thankfully, the vast majority of us will not have experiences like Zechariah or Ebenezer Scrooge, but we should take heed nonetheless. Let Zechariah's response be a warning to those of us who wait with patience for a season only to rush to sin soon after. May it help us remember to see God's character in his word and seek God's presence through prayerful faith and obedience, trusting that his word is true and his truth is good.

— Day 4 —

Proclamation
Part I

When the appointed time drew near, mighty Gabriel appeared
In the town of Nazareth to Mary, the virgin betrothed to Joseph

LUKE 1:26-33

When you ask someone about their favorite Christmas memory, a particular scene may spring to mind. For some, it is set somewhere in their childhood home, perhaps sitting on the floor in a living room with stockings hanging in front of a warm hearth. Others will think fondly of visiting a relative's house and sharing a meal at their dining room table. Still others cling to recent memories of Christmas mornings spent creating newer, wonderful traditions. Few will have memories of Christmas mornings spent atop the Empire State Building or on the rim of the Grand Canyon. Why? It seems as if the value in our special holiday memories does not just come from remarkable spaces but from the time spent with the people we love.

This should not surprise most of us regarding our Christmas memories, but why do we treat so much of the rest of our lives this way? Why do we try to make mansions of each daily comfort and find dramatic grandeur in every moment?

In the coming of Jesus, the God of heavenly mansions and grandeur makes his presence known in a shockingly average place.

After delivering a message to the priest Zechariah in the great city of Jerusalem, the angel Gabriel goes out to a town called Nazareth. The same holy God whose presence had hovered over the ark in Solomon's temple and filled the tent of meeting in the days of Moses now makes himself known to a virgin girl in a small town. The people of that time described Nazareth like this: "Could anything good come from there?"[1] The saying is like Nebraska's recent slogan: "Honestly, it's not for everyone." (It's real! Look it up.)

Some twenty-four generations before Mary was born, the prophet Elijah encountered God's presence in a similar way. While taking refuge from persecution in a mountain cave, God's presence appeared to him. Elijah saw a violent wind tear through rocks as the mountain shook and fire flashed before him, but at the end of it all, he heard a low whisper.

The Bible says that God was not in the wind, the earthquake, or the fire, but in that small voice.[2] God's quiet voice there is not a sign of weakness. Elsewhere in Scripture he has spoken mightily from each: wind, earthquake, and fire. No, God is not weak, but he demonstrates his strength through his faithful presence in even the lowest places—yes, even in a virgin's womb in Nazareth.

Though Gabriel appears to the humble Mary in this lowly place, he calls her by a majestic title: "O favored one!" He even reinforces the idea after Mary responds in fear, reassuring her that she has found favor with God. We may be tempted to try to discover what Mary did to deserve such a title and favor. Was she especially pious? Was she the most righteous in her small town? Was she the most trusting of the Lord in her family? We certainly see great faith and merit in Mary's life, but that is not Gabriel's meaning.

This particular Greek word for "favored one" appears only one other time in the New Testament. In Ephesians 1:5-6, Paul uses it to describe God's grace toward us, saying that God lovingly chose us "for adoption to himself as sons through Jesus Christ, according to the purpose of his will, to the praise of his glorious grace, with which *he has blessed us* in

---

1   John 1:46
2   1 Kings 19:11-12

the Beloved." Behind that simple phrase, *"he has blessed us,"* is the very same title that Gabriel gave to Mary: "favored one." Paul means that the presence and purpose of God in Mary's life to send Jesus to this earth is the very same expression of God's love to seek out and adopt a lowly people to become children in his family.

In that sense, Gabriel's announcement to Mary is also for us. Do you feel spiritually orphaned by your sin and the brokenness of the world? Turn to faith in Jesus. For all who believe in his name, he gives "the right to become children of God."[3] All of us who believe in Jesus have found that despite our failings and rebellion against God, he has come to us. He has found us in the smallest towns and forgotten corners of the world to adopt us, to make us his sons and daughters. Though we were at our lowest, God "raised us up with him and seated us with him in the heavenly places in Christ Jesus, so that in the coming ages he might show the immeasurable riches of his grace in kindness toward us."[4]

Do you expect to find God in the lowest places? Do you treat the daily mundanity of your life with the same expectation of God's presence and purpose? Christian, beware the siren's song of material success, fame, and thrills associated with faith in Jesus. That is not his Spirit's regular abode. If the life of Jesus teaches us anything about the Christian life, it is that radical faith comes from unimpressive people in mediocre places. Ours is a faith proven more by humble, daily rhythms than by rare, dramatic performances.

Find God's grace this Advent as you seek Christ in the lowest places. Just as he came to Nazareth, so he comes to you, wherever you are.

---

3   John 1:12
4   Ephesians 2:6-7

Proclamation
Part II

He will be great
He will be known
As the Son of the Most High
And He will reign forever

2 SAMUEL 7:1-17

I genuinely enjoy wrapping Christmas gifts. I have some favorite old boxes and bows that I like to use year after year, and I love choosing different wrapping paper that fits the gift or the recipient in some way. Of course, the danger in a well-wrapped gift is that it may obscure the true value of the item within. How many of us have opened up a beautifully wrapped gift only to discover a disappointing present!

When Gabriel announces the good news about Mary's son, he includes the titles and accreditations of this child, but they are not like Christmas wrapping paper. They are not mere ceremonial names, as if God needs empty titles and designations in order to be honored and revered, as if Jesus is a mediocre gift wrapped in shiny bows and paper.

On the contrary, each title is given as a testimony to God's real power to bring about salvation for his people. This is a not a son who must live up to his family name, but a family name which would have no power or meaning without this son.

God declares that his son will be called by the name "Jesus." Our society is well-acquainted with the word for various reasons. We hear it used as a blasphemous curse or a reckless exclamation. In several modern cultures, the name is still used quite commonly. This was also the case in Mary's day, but God was not simply choosing a conventional name to show solidarity with the Hebrew people. God gave him the name, "Jesus," because it means, "God saves."

The apostle Peter declares rightly in Acts 4:12, "and there is salvation in no one else, for there is no other name under heaven given among men by which we must be saved." God is so intentional with the name of Jesus that he makes it exclusive for salvation! Jesus alone brought about God's ultimate salvation for the lost when he came to serve, suffer, and die on the cross. Though humanity is enslaved by sin and doomed to the wrath of hell, the cross of Jesus breaks the chains and sets captives free. All who repent and believe in him will be truly and completely saved.

God also declares that Mary's son Jesus will also be called the "son of the Most High." Certainly, being from heaven, Jesus comes from the place of greatest honor, privilege, and power. He therefore has the authority to bring an irrevocable salvation for his people, a gift that cannot be take away once received.

More than that, Gabriel also means to say that Jesus is the only son of God himself. In the Old Testament, God alone is called the "Most High," being the only eternal Creator who is highest in glory, honor, wisdom, and strength. This striking declaration reveals that Jesus is not just *a* son of God, like some Greek demigod or other partial divinity, but he *is* God. Like a son shares the full title of his surname with his father, so Jesus shares all the same glory and personhood of his divine father. He is the one eternal Creator himself, "for in him, all the fullness of God was pleased to dwell."[1]

Lastly, God declares that his son Jesus will receive his ancestor David's throne and promised eternal kingdom. In 2 Samuel 7, King David sought to build a house for God. Up

---

1   Colossians 1:19

to that point, the place of God's presence dwelt in a tent. But David recognized that God alone was Most High, the true king over his people, and was deserving of the utmost honor and worship. He wanted to build a temple where God's presence would dwell permanently, where his name would be honored and magnified, but Nathan the prophet responded to David's request with a surprising promise.

Rather than build it in his lifetime, God would give David a son to construct such a house, and God would bless David and his kingship through a remarkable covenant. He declares that he will establish David's throne, house, and kingdom forever, for the good of God's people and for God's own glory.

Just as God called the humble King David out of serving in a pasture into a majestic palace, he now calls Mary out of girlhood in a small town into a queenly motherhood in the divine palace of heaven. Her son Jesus carries a family name and title with global implications far beyond Mary's time and generation. One day, this king will return to establish his forever kingdom in full on this earth, gathering into that same divine palace every humble citizen of his kingdom, everyone who has believed in his name.

Especially as we celebrate Advent, we should live in anticipation of that day and put our faith in Jesus, the only one whose name will endure for eternity. Until that day, we should remember that there are still many cultures who do not know this name of God's son and forever king. Those of us who have experienced his salvation should long to see his name taken to those who do not yet know him.

How might your gifts and prayers advance his name this season? To whom has God sent you to share this name? This Christmas, let us not follow in the footsteps of those who work in vain to build a name for themselves, but serve in the kingdom that will last forever, under the king whose very name means salvation.

Proclamation
Part III

How can this be, if what you say is true?
How can I bear to carry the weight of this great child?
With man it is impossible
But nothing's impossible with God

LUKE 1:34-38

When my friend Preston and I were working on the first few songs of this album years ago, we wrestled with how to understand the difference between Zechariah's and Mary's questions. Why did Gabriel respond to one with scolding and silencing but the other with further explanation and encouragement?

Every word we speak reflects a reality in our hearts. Jesus would teach on this several chapters after this story, saying, "The good person out of the good treasure of his heart produces good, and the evil person out of his evil treasure produces evil, for out of the abundance of the heart his mouth speaks."[1]

Luke wants Theophilus—and us, his readers—to have a clear understanding of the difference between Zechariah and Mary's hearts on the basis of belief. For Zechariah, Gabriel explicitly tells him: "you will be silent and unable to speak... because *you did not believe* my words."[2] For Mary, it is Elizabeth who later declares, "blessed is *she who believed* that there would be a fulfillment of what was spoken to her from the Lord."[3]

---

1   Luke 6:45
2   Luke 1:20
3   Luke 1:45

In their responses, Luke shows us how our beliefs determine our attitudes, actions, and ultimately, our fates—but we can also learn this from their questions.

Both questions continue Luke's theme of certainty found at the beginning of his book, yet with subtle clues as to their contrasting motivations. Zechariah essentially asks, "how can I *really know* this for certain? The circumstances are too impossible!" Mary, on the other hand, asks, "How will this *certainly happen*?" or, "How *can this be*, since I have not known a man?"

Catch the difference? It's subtle, for sure, especially when partially obscured by our English translations. Zechariah's question reveals his lack of belief that what Gabriel has announced will really happen. As discussed on Day 3, his prior faith in God is set aside in a moment of unbelief as Zechariah doubts that God would or even could ever really give him a child. Mary's question, on the other hand, reveals a pure heart of faith.

It shouldn't surprise us, then, to see that Gabriel responds to Zechariah with rebuke but to Mary with a testimony of God's actions and miraculous power. Luke employs a play on words here to make this point. Linguistically, Zechariah's "lack of knowing" has to do with his unbelief, but Mary's "lack of knowing" has to do with her purity as a virgin. In a great reversal of cultural expectations, we see the faith of this young virgin eclipse that of an old priest. "While man looks at the outward appearance, God looks at the heart."[4] We would do well to follow in the faith of Mary when facing seemingly impossible circumstances, believing the word of the angel Gabriel that "nothing is impossible with God."

Still, we might think, wouldn't it have been culturally easier for Mary to conceive after completing her formal betrothal, or after having a couple kids and getting experience as a mother?

---

4 1 Samuel 16:7

The wonder of God's mysterious, immaculate conception in Mary's womb isn't just a mythological footnote in her life or the biblical narrative. Jesus being born of a virgin presents striking implications for every believer. Paul writes about this in 1 Corinthians 15:47-48, saying, "The first man was from the earth, a man of dust; the second man is from heaven. As was the man of dust, so also are those who are of the dust, and as is the man of heaven, so also are those who are of heaven." Adam, the first man, the man of dust, was also a man of sin, and all of those born in his line have inherited it. Thus, salvation from sin and spiritual death is impossible in human terms.

But Jesus, the man of heaven, is a man of God's own righteousness, and all of those born in him inherit it. When we come to faith in him, God transforms our hearts and gives us miraculous spiritual life where no life could formerly exist. The virgin birth we celebrate each Christmas gives us hope that we also, though we have all doubted like Zechariah, might believe like Mary and inherit the same life of heaven.

If we're honest, we often wonder whether God's plan is really so wise. Won't it be easier to step out in faith once we know how things will turn out? Won't it be easier to follow God on this journey with more assurance of success or finances or help? Won't it be easier to trust God without this particular situation, sickness, weakness, pain, or struggle? This story reminds us that God not only knows our every weakness; he knows the way in which his miraculous power will redeem it for good. May God increase our faith to be like Mary's so that we will remember God's sovereign power in even the most daunting and impossible situations.

Son of David

Part I

Oh God, what do I do with this horrible news?

MATTHEW 1:18-25

G od has a strange way of surprising his people in his perfect timing and giving clarity and empathy in ways that we could never imagine. For example, I'm writing this particular devotional the day after my wife and I suddenly discovered that she is five months pregnant. (Yes, you read that right.) Without going into the details, we discovered that she was pregnant with our 22-week old baby boy during a shocking yet joy-filled sonogram. As you can imagine, our sudden discovery resulted in all kinds of fun but awkward conversations.

Poor Joseph must have also had some awkward conversations with his family and friends after discovering Mary's pregnancy. When the people who knew about their betrothal found out, they must have been shocked and disappointed in both of them.

To be honest, they had some right to feel that way. When a woman has a child not only out of wedlock, but by another man besides her betrothed, it exposes layers of sin that affect marriages, families, and communities. Perhaps you've had to deal with these kinds of situations without the hope of an answer. Life is messy and broken and complicated because of sin, but of course, just as in Joseph's life, God shows us immense grace in these situations. Through repentance and a journey of faith, God can turn even the most awkward and sinful of situations into beautiful blessings of joy.

Mary's fiancé Joseph showed great faith in an awkward and difficult situation. In this brief detour from Luke's account, we can see how Joseph walked by faith through this situation in the book of Matthew. There, the author describes him as a "just man," unwilling to put Mary to shame. Because of this, Joseph resolves to divorce Mary quietly.[1]

We don't know any more details than that, but in the midst of what seemed like an entirely unjust situation, we know Joseph acted justly toward Mary. This is no small thing. Though the situation should have brought great shame, Joseph worked to avoid shaming Mary. Though it should have brought severe and immediate judgment, Joseph showed patience and mercy.

Joseph's character is a shadow of the selfless, sacrificial love found in his son Jesus. Though entirely innocent, Jesus endured the shame we deserved because of our sin when he suffered and died on the cross. When Paul writes to the church in Rome about the suffering Jesus endured for us, he highlights the injustice we have inflicted on both God and the world. Unlike Joseph in this situation, we deserve judgment from God for our sin, but in the cross of Jesus, we are "justified by his grace as a gift, through the redemption that is in Christ."[2] In his divine righteousness, God transformed the earthly injustice of the cross into eternal justice for all believers, "so that he might be just and the justifier of the one who has faith in Jesus."[3]

Friend, if you fear any awkward conversation with God about your sin, don't put your hope in your own solutions. Joseph acted justly, but God would step in immediately after to bring an even better justice through his son. Trust in the justice of God in the cross of Jesus which atones for sin and removes all shame. Because of his loving work on the cross and the gift of faith, God's eternal posture toward those who

---

1   Matthew 1:19
2   Romans 3:24
3   Romans 3:26

believe in him is unwavering love and mercy. God's justice doesn't just quietly deal with your sin and move on, but boldly and finally forgives you and calls you into a relationship with himself. You can trust him—even more than any spouse, family member, or friend—because he loves you.

Jesus is the only truly just man. He calls all who believe in him to submit to his righteous judgments. He endured shame, suffering, and the pain of death so that we might share in his heavenly fellowship with the Father. Let us reflect his divine justice and preach his gospel so that every measure of guilt and shame might be removed from our own hearts, and from our world.

Son of David
Part II

For everything that's happening is happening for a reason
"Behold, the virgin shall conceive and bear Immanuel"

ISAIAH 7:10-17 & 8:5-17

We've all heard the saying, "everything happens for a reason." We hear it repeated all year round, but the Christmas season is filled to the brim with such sentiments. Quick, positive sayings dominate signs, slogans, and cards. "Believe in the magic of Christmas," or, "Love comes down at Christmas," or, "May all your Christmas dreams come true!"

There is a kernel of truth in many of these hopeful sayings, but we need to dig deeper to find any real meaning or hope in them. Do dreams come true even when plans fail and bank accounts empty? Does true love still come when loved ones abandon? Is there really a reason for the horrible incident, the painful illness, or the tragic death?

In the previous devotional, we looked at the how Joseph acted justly in the midst of a difficult situation, as mentioned in Matthew 1:19. We would do well to note the significance of the phrase that immediately follows in verse 20: "he considered these things." Matthew does not describe Joseph as hasty but as one who considers, even in a time of stress and trouble.

Joseph only had a handful of months, even weeks, to make a decision about Mary's inexplicable pregnancy. In the midst of that season of waiting and wrestling, God graciously sends an angel to him in a dream who explains Mary's miraculous conception and tells him not to fear and to take Mary as his wife. In verse 24, Joseph's response gives us another glimpse of his character: "he did as the angel of the Lord commanded him."

We should aspire to be like Joseph in this. Whatever doubts, questions, and concerns he had, he trusted what God called him to do beyond his own understanding. The "reason" that gave him confidence and peace wasn't based on what brought him the most comfort, the quickest answer, or the greatest success. No, Joseph recognized the sovereign might of God in his revelation, and like his wife Mary, he seemed to be able to say in response, "I am a servant of the Lord; let it be to me according to your word."[1]

God's answer certainly gave Joseph some confidence in his present situation, as he learned "that which is conceived in her is from the Holy Spirit." But if we could put ourselves in the shoes (or sandals) of this first-century, small-town Jewish man pledged to a woman who becomes unexpectedly pregnant, we would realize the questions and doubts that remain. What about their families? Their friends? Their reputations? These were all questions of concern for Joseph, yet he trusted and obeyed the voice of the Lord.

Yes, "everything happens for a reason," but the reason does not guarantee comfort, ease, or success.

Matthew's gospel is filled with Old Testament references that proclaim Jesus as the Messiah, God's anointed one promised long ago across many centuries by the prophets of Israel. In his opening narrative, Matthew inserts the first of eighteen prophecies which prove that Jesus is the promised Messiah, Savior, and Son of God. As we discussed previously on day 6, the miraculous conception of Jesus carries great implications. Here, Matthew reminds us that as wild as the situation seemed, it was foretold by prophecy.

Long ago, the Holy Spirit spoke through the prophet Isaiah. God sent him to speak to the idolatrous and wicked King Ahaz

---

1 Luke 1:38

when he found himself in the midst of trouble and distress from his enemies. He told him that he should repent and trust in the Lord's sign and help. Unlike Joseph, Ahaz ultimately turned away from God to himself and his idols for help.

Despite that, the Lord promised a sign that a virgin was coming to bear a son called "Immanuel," God with us. The same prophecy which pronounced judgment to Ahaz brought comfort for Joseph in the midst of his distress. The same prophecy that once revealed a lack of God's presence in Israel long ago now brought the glorious revelation of his presence into the lives of Mary, Joseph, and the entire world.

Through this prophecy, Joseph came to understand that the presence and work of God brings salvation to those who believe and terror to those who do not. Jesus himself is the cornerstone and sure foundation for those who believe in him and a stumbling block of offense to those who do not.[2]

What about you? Is Jesus more like a temporary help, a tool to use when it works for the situation, or is he your lifelong savior, one worth trusting in no matter what life brings? Joseph could trust in this Jesus because God's presence was at work, not only literally in Mary's womb, but spiritually in his own life. The promise of the incarnation gave him confidence through faith in God before he ever saw Jesus in the flesh.

For those of us who believe in Jesus, his incarnation should not just be a seasonal wonder of remembering God coming to earth as a baby. The incarnation of Jesus is the breathtaking, atoning, unifying, eternal, and only comfort for our weary world. The promises of God in Scripture should ring loudly in our ears as we cling to the hope of his saving presence this Advent. No matter what trials and troubles we will face, we can live with patient trust in Jesus, who is Immanuel, the God who is with us. Is there any better reason?

---

2   1 Peter 2:4-10

Wonder
Part I

When Elizabeth saw her walk up
The promised baby in her jumped for joy

LUKE 1:39-45

In Texas, Christmastime is not nearly as dark or as cold as in most other parts of the Northern Hemisphere. Nevertheless, you'll still find us celebrating the season with the same depictions of warmth and light in a dark, snowy landscape.

As a kid, I always loved setting up our Christmas lights outside. We would wrap all of our trees and line the sidewalk with strands of warm white light. We would hoist a bright star up to the second floor level with strands of blue light streaming to the ground like starlight, all draped behind a quaint nativity scene. Even if it was 75 degrees outside on Christmas Eve, our house lit up like a beacon of warmth on a cold, dark night.

From the outside, the virgin Mary did not look so radiant as she traveled down from Nazareth to the hill country to visit her cousin, Elizabeth, but don't miss the significance of this scene. Miles away, the priests were continuing to offer ritual sacrifices at the altar of God, the place where his holy presence had once dwelt in full glory in the days of King Solomon. They worshiped God at the temple in Jerusalem, longing for his presence to once again fill that place with the majesty of those ancient days. Some did so faithfully, but many pursued their own interests and traditions. Either way, a materialistic culture of greed and hypocrisy was allowed to fester in the place God intended to be a center for prayer and worship for the nations.

At this same moment in history, while all these priests were serving in the city of Jerusalem, Mary walked out into the hill country carrying the living presence of God in her womb like a lantern in the dark.

Likewise, our lives may be filled with ritual and the appearance of worship, yet remain empty and lifeless—but when you come to Jesus through repentance and faith, he draws even closer to you than what Mary experienced.

Humble Christian, "do you not know that your body is a temple of the Holy Spirit within you, whom you have from God?"[1] God's grace in saving us does a miraculous work of renovation in our souls which transforms them from dilapidated tombs into houses of worship. These houses, which are our very lives, are where God's own Spirit delights to dwell. Whatever our outside appearance and circumstances may be, the presence of God in our lives should inspire Christ-centered worship in the hearts of fellow believers. After all, that's what temples are truly for: worship!

Is that true of you? Is your life increasingly hospitable to the presence and work of God's Spirit? Are your character, attitude, schedule, and priorities centers for godly worship in your corner of the world? Are you, like Mary, a humble lantern in the dark?

When Mary approaches her destination, Elizabeth's womb leaps to worship in the presence of God. The last time two unborn children responded to one another from the womb, it was the twin sons of Isaac—Jacob and Esau—wrestling with one another in Rebekah's womb. Rebekah inquired of the Lord in Genesis 25 and learned that this foretold a rivalry, struggle, and opposition between them. That certainly played out in their young lives, marked by competition and strife rather than worship to God.

---

1   1 Corinthians 6:19

But not so for the baby in Elizabeth's womb! He responds to the Christ child with submissive, trembling worship, a harmonious subjugation born out of peace and joy rather than envy and strife. Like the seas and the mountains mentioned in Psalm 114, the unborn prophet of God leaps in his holy presence to worship the one who made him.

This joyous act of worship is not just some frivolous dance in the womb. It's an act of spiritual war.

The same word used to describe the leaping of John in Elizabeth's womb only occurs in only one other place in the New Testament. The other time it appears is also in Luke, and the phrase is also translated "leap for joy," but in a very different context. Jesus is teaching his followers about how the world will treat them for worshiping him. He tells them: "Blessed are you when people hate you and when they exclude you and revile you and spurn your name as evil, on account of the Son of Man! Rejoice in that day, and *leap for joy*, for behold, your reward is great in heaven; for so their fathers did to the prophets."[2]

Jesus promises that the world will respond with hate, exclusion, censure, and rejection to the sacrificial worship of his saving kingship. How often have our own hearts reviled Christ in this way! If you find yourself more opposed to Jesus than joyously submissive, consider the hope and the promise of his salvation. Will you submit to worship him? Only he can bring the eternal life, joy, and peace that he purchased through his cross and resurrection.

For those of us who have submitted to him, do we count this Jesus as worthy of such joy when hate is the response? Friends and neighbors, no matter the response, your community needs to hear that there is a hope worth celebrating this season, for the days are short. Parents, your children need to see you worship Jesus, for you can give them no greater gift.

---

2   Luke 6:22-23

Brothers and sisters, our world needs to see the light of the glory of Christ in us, for who else will show them?

Mary and Elizabeth knew that the world held no better joy than Christ, the only one worthy of our submission and worship. Even brighter than the lights we display this Christmas season, may our worship also reflect the light of God's glory and the great joy of Christ's good news.

Wonder
Part II

Why would God grant this to me?
I know I don't deserve a thing
But blessed is the God who keeps his promise
Blessed is the one he's sent to save us

LUKE 11:27-28

Everyone exchanges Christmas gifts a little differently. Some families celebrate a Christmas morning visit from Santa. Others give all their gifts on Christmas Eve. Some play gift games, others assign "Secret Santas." Some make detailed lists, others like surprises.

However we do it, the goal is always to leave a big impression of joy and gratitude. We can picture familiar scenes of kids screaming and jumping after getting their favorite toy and adults hugging and crying over an especially thoughtful gift.

In every situation, no matter how much we may try to fake it, our honest reaction reveals our true attitude toward the gift. The Bible teaches us that there is no greater gift than Jesus, and in Luke's account of his coming, we see one of the most incredible reactions from one of the most unlikely people.

It seems like the first person outside of Jesus's immediate family to hear of his birth was formerly barren, elderly Elizabeth. Her husband Zechariah had caught a glimpse of God's plan when he heard the promise of a prophet son, but he had responded in unbelief and was made mute. Elizabeth, on the other hand, recognized the power of God at work in her life, even early on in her pregnancy.[1] Thoughts of Psalm

---

1   Luke 1:24-25

139:13 may have sprung to Elizabeth's mind as she marveled at God's miraculous power to create life even in her old age. This acknowledgement of God's power clearly became a pattern for her life, as we see when Mary comes to visit her.

When the Spirit-conceived womb of Mary approaches the Spirit-opened womb of Elizabeth, Elizabeth responds with unbridled worship. Though God had shut the priest's mouth for disobedience, God opened his wife's mouth in Spirit-filled worship.

Throughout human history, we are often tempted to see external wealth, status, and position as our reason for worth. We are also tempted to find internal value by prioritizing ourselves above others and resisting the need for help and change, but Jesus knows us for who we truly are.

In our sinfulness, we all need forgiveness and help, no matter what our lives might look like. We should be challenged by Elizabeth's humble cry in Luke 1:43, when she asks, "And why is this granted to me that the mother of my Lord should come to me?" The people around Jesus would often grumble when he spent time with the people they saw as lesser, but Jesus corrected them in Luke 19:10, saying, "for the Son of Man came to seek and to save the lost." Only those who understand their lostness can truly understand the heart of Jesus and, believing in him, find true salvation.

Elizabeth also blessed Mary for believing in the Lord: "And blessed is she who believed that there would be a fulfillment of what was spoken to her from the Lord."[2] We can imagine the encouragement both women must have felt at these words. Elizabeth's promised son fulfills his prophetic role by pointing his mother to Jesus, even from the womb! When Elizabeth worships God this way, it brings comfort and confirmation to Mary on her journey of faith.

---

2   Luke 1:45

Jesus himself would teach about this kind of true worship and faith. At one point during his ministry, he encountered an excited woman who was clearly moved by his teaching. She understood that Jesus was teaching the things of God with amazing clarity and accuracy. Luke records her telling him, "Blessed is the womb that bore you, and the breasts at which you nursed!"[3]

At first glance, this seems to be a great response, one that sounds pretty similar to Elizabeth's, but Jesus's response shows otherwise. Rather than respond with gratitude and affirmation, Jesus corrects her. He tells her, "'Blessed rather are those who hear the word of God and keep it!'"[4] His hope is not just that she would just recognize blessing in someone else from a distance, but hear God's blessing in his word, believe it in faith, and obey it herself.

Though Mary and Elizabeth shared wonderful titles and experiences as women, relatives, and pregnant mothers of promised babies, it is their bond of faith which made them truly blessed. All earthly blessings pale in comparison to knowing God as Father through saving faith in his Son and indwelling life through his Spirit. This greatest blessing comes by grace through faith, when those who realize they are poor in spirit turn in faith to find their greatest blessing in the God who came to save them. This is what truly ignites a life of worship which honors God and blesses others. It all begins with understanding the immeasurable value of Jesus.

There is no greater gift.

---

3 Luke 11:27
4 Luke 11:28

— Day 11 —

O Soul Rejoice
Part I

For he has remembered his child
Rejoice!

LUKE 1:46-56

Outside of churches and concerts, it seems like people in our culture sing together at only a few different occasions: birthdays, sporting events, and Christmas. In each case, the goal is the same: to celebrate. At a birthday party, we celebrate another year of someone's life. At a sporting event, we cheer on our favorite team to victory. But at Christmastime, what are we really celebrating?

The traditional lyrics to "Jingle Bells" celebrate a fun sleigh ride. (The non-traditional lyrics lament some unfortunate circumstances for Batman.) "Rudolph the Red-Nosed Reindeer" celebrates a classic underdog story. "Deck the Halls," "Sleigh Ride," "Santa Claus is Coming to Town," and "Have Yourself a Merry Little Christmas" are all pretty self-explanatory.

When we sing along with all of these different songs, we're simply having fun and celebrating this strangely wonderful and nostalgic season that we observe every year. This lighthearted celebration is loads of fun! (Trust me, I start singing Christmas songs the day after Thanksgiving, at the latest.) But when this haphazard sentimentality bleeds into other areas of our lives, we come dangerously close to worshiping Christmas over its Christ.

When Mary bursts into song after visiting Elizabeth, she celebrates something very specific and intentional. Her words of praise echo Psalm 103, the song of her ancestor David, in which he sings, "Bless the Lord, O my soul, and all that is within me, bless his holy name!"[1]

In our English translations of the Bible, the soul is mentioned in the Psalms more than in any other book. Most of the time, we read the psalmists crying out from the depths of their soul in anguish or entrusting their soul to God for help in times of trouble. But notably, in Psalm 103, David calls upon his soul, or his whole being, to bless the Lord. David does so from remembering God's character which he declared to his people, the very same words used to communicate God's name in the Old Testament: "The Lord is merciful and gracious, slow to anger and abounding in steadfast love."[2]

Mary takes much of the language and idea behind David's psalm and applies it to her own life and experience. She erupts in praise to God because she has seen his character in action, bringing his mercy, grace, and love into the world in her own life. She understood that God was bringing salvation to the world when he called her to be the mother of his king. Just as Gabriel had instructed Mary to name this king Jesus, "God saves," so in her song of praise, she praises God as her savior. Just as Gabriel had called her "favored one," she praises God for looking upon her "humble estate." Just as Gabriel promised that Jesus would be king forever, she praises God for bringing about a blessing that will endure through all generations. And that's all just in the first couple verses!

We will unpack the later verses of Mary's song in the following devotional, but even in this opening, it is clear that Mary responded in worship because she understood what God had done and was doing in her life. Mary recognized the salvation that her son Jesus would bring. If you are beginning to recognize Jesus in this way for the first time, God is also at

---

1   Psalm 103:1
2   Psalm 103:8

work in your heart. Recognize the gift that God has given in Christ and become a lifelong worshiper of him.

Mary's song of praise helps us understand how to sing not only at Advent and Christmastime, but in every season. When we sing in worship to God, our primary motivation is not an arbitrary time on the clock or the season's passing whims. Our primary motivation is rooted in God's saving work in sending Christ to live a perfect life, die a sacrificial death, and rise from the grave—all to save us! When we believe and walk by faith in Jesus, we can truly sing with Mary, "He has done great things *for me*." Every rediscovery and reminder of that good news should be the catalyst for our worship through song.

Mary personally and intimately experienced the magnitude of God's grace in her life. For all of us who have believed in Jesus for salvation, we have also shared in this glorious experience, so we can also rejoice.

What does your soul magnify most during this season? From the depths of your inner self, what is the object of your greatest hope and source of joy? Christian, is it not Jesus? What would it look like for you to respond in praise to his salvation?

O soul: rejoice!

— Day 12 —

O Soul Rejoice
Part II

O Israel, rejoice!
Rejoice, rejoice!

ISAIAH 41

Writing a song based on another song written by a person in Scripture who also based her song on another song written by a person in Scripture is intimidating, to say the least. (It's also hard to write.) Writing that same song for your wife to sing is even more intimidating!

That said, I truly enjoyed writing "O Soul Rejoice."It's one of my favorite songs on the record. I chose the title of the song from Mary's opening line, as have many others. But upon further reflection, I think if Mary had chosen a title for her own song, she would have picked, "The Servant of the Lord."

Mary refers to herself as a servant twice in Luke: once when responding in submissive faith to the angel Gabriel and again at the beginning of her song.[1] But she ends her song in reference to another servant: the people of Israel.

To highlight this difference, Luke records two different Greek words for 'servant.' The word found in verses 38 and 48 is *doulē*, which refers to a personal handmaiden or bondservant. Mary is using it in this personal manner to identify herself as one who is in complete submissive service to God, her master. As we looked at in yesterday's devotional, Mary understands that God and his salvation in Jesus is very personal to her. But when she calls Israel God's servant in verse 54, we see a

---

1   Luke 1:38 & 48, respectively

different word: *pais*, which describes a young manservant, like a young boy in service to a king.

Look at Isaiah 41:8-10. Here, God himself identifies Israel as his servant.

"But you, Israel, my servant,
 Jacob, whom I have chosen,
  the offspring of Abraham, my friend;
you whom I took from the ends of the earth,
  and called from its farthest corners,
saying to you, 'You are my servant,
 I have chosen you and not cast you off';
fear not, for I am with you;
 be not dismayed, for I am your God;
I will strengthen you, I will help you,
 I will uphold you with my righteous right hand."

The people of Israel referenced in Isaiah 41 were afraid of the nations raging and warring against them, but God reminded them his might and power. His strength exceeds that of any nation or people, yet for those who are his servant, he comes not to dismay or destroy but to save. When God calls them his servant, "my friend," he reminds them of the way he protects, upholds, strengthens, helps, and loves his people.

Mary realizes that God has not only saved her personally, but communally. The baby in her womb is way that God will save his people, just like he promised in Isaiah 41. She sings confidently about God and his salvation for his people. He saves them mightily from their enemies and provides them with everything they need. He scatters the proud, exalts the lowly, and remembers his every promise. *This* is the God of Israel of whom Mary sings.

In our efforts to sing praises to God, we must be careful not to let lesser definitions of him corrupt our worship. This is God's point to his people later in Isaiah 41 when he warns them that their idols and lesser gods "are a delusion; their works are nothing."[2] Not remembering God's grace and mercy will lead us to sing to a god who will not forgive, who loves to reject and exact harsh punishment. Not remembering God's patience will lead us to sing to a god who acts quickly for our own benefit. Not remembering God's covenantal love and faithfulness will lead us to sing to a distant god who has no care for our petty troubles. Not remembering God's holy justice will lead us to sing to a god who has no concern for sin and its punishment, individual or corporate. We must take care to remember the truth of who God is, what he has done, and for whom he has done it.

When God sent Jesus, he was not fulfilling the wishes of a handful of individuals or honoring his promises to a few. God was making good on all of the promises he had made to the whole remnant of his faithful servant Israel. And just like Mary reminds us, "from Abraham to his offspring forever," God's work in Israel was always intended as a blessing for all nations.[3] Anyone who understands the majesty of God's king of salvation may, like Mary, bow the knee and become a worshiping servant in his kingdom.

It has been said before, our faith in Christ is personal, but it is not private. The hope of Christmas cannot be observed or understood alone. As long as you have believers in Jesus in your community, God has called you to worship him this Christmas with them, to worship as a servant together with his people.

---

2   Isaiah 41:29
3   Genesis 12:2, 17:4-7, 18:17-18

On the Horizon
Part I

But God showed his tender mercy
When you, my son, arrived
He gave me my voice again

READ LUKE 1:57-66

The Lord has been kind to me in that I cannot think of a Christmas spent without my family. This season has been rich with traditions for me since I was young, and I love getting to spend it with loved ones. Whether that is your experience in the past or your hope for the future, there is something biblically sweet, warm, and encouraging about spending time over the holidays with family.

But (you knew this was coming), that all can change in an instant. However peaceful our Christmas card pictures appear, we know that peace isn't always the norm. Sometimes you have to spend weeks on end trying to make plans only for everyone to come together for a couple tense hours. Sometimes you try and organize a nice family meal that devolves into a kitchen nightmare or a text group chat argument over who's bringing what. Sometimes sudden disaster or bad news wreaks havoc on your family and your lives are so turned around that every plan you made comes crashing to the ground.

When Zechariah and Elizabeth gave birth to their son, family came from all around to celebrate. At first, Luke paints a beautiful picture of this in Luke 1:58. "Neighbors and relatives heard that the Lord had shown great mercy to her, and they rejoiced with her." This is what God's family looks like: a group of people who love to praise God for his mercy shown in each other's lives. What an encouragement!

But Zechariah felt some pressure and struggle with his family at the birth of his first son. No doubt, many came from all around to celebrate this miraculous birth, and they praised God for his mercy. However, the sound of praise quickly devolved into a clamor as their presumption about the name of the child overtook their praise to God. You can imagine the noise of voices that rose to announce their opinions over one another. However well-intentioned, their voices were about to become a living example of God's admonition: "For my thoughts are not your thoughts, neither are your ways my ways, declares the Lord."[1]

Thankfully, one family member at this gathering was ready to boldly declare the truth. Elizabeth spoke up above the noise to announce God's name for her son: "No; he shall be called John."What an example! Christian, when you are gathered with your family, be like Elizabeth. When there's any question in the conversation that pertains to the truth of God, don't be afraid to speak it. Whether you're young or old, guest or host, eloquent or inarticulate, God can use any voice to turn the hearts of his people.

But still, the family was not convinced. Luke summarizes the logic behind the family's disagreement for us: "None of your relatives is called by this name."[2]

Mary had previously sung boldly of the character of God, who remembered mercy for his people and was making good on his promises. Luke, the great storyteller, shifts our focus back to silent old Zechariah. His mouth had been shut for at least nine months, ever since the day when he heard God's plan to give him a son and did not believe him. But Gabriel had promised that Zechariah's mouth would be opened again on the day that this son would be born. The God who Mary

---

1   Isaiah 55:8
2   Luke 1:61

just praised for remembering his promises is about to prove his faithfulness once again.

The family handed Zechariah a tablet to write on, and he wrote clearly and faithfully: "His name is John." At that moment, Luke tells us that his tongue was loosed and he immediately began speaking, blessing God. Finally, the man of God who formerly doubted the word of God is seen speaking the truth of God to those around him.

Have your Christmas celebrations been more self-focused and chaotic than you'd like to admit? Could it be that you have placed your attention and focus on the earthly over the eternal? When there was confusion among the disciples about their lives after death, Jesus said, "I am the way, the truth, and the life. No one comes to the Father except through me."[3] Do you believe this?

I love how Luke records the response of Zechariah's family and friends gathered there: holy fear. When God interjects his truth into the world through faithful witnesses, people don't respond according to the stature of the man or woman speaking, but according to God himself.

For so many of us, God has given us some measure of opportunity to spend time with our families and loved ones during the Christmas season. Take advantage of these times and enjoy them! Celebrate Christmas together by celebrating the mercy of God in sending Christ, but when things get tense or frustrating or wearisome this season, don't run from the opportunity. Boldly speak the truth and stand with humble confidence in Christ, and see how God might use it for your family's good and his glory.

---

3   John 14:6

── Day 14 ──

On the Horizon
Part II

Blessed, blessed be the Lord of Israel
For he promised Abraham, as well
As our fathers and prophets did tell

LUKE 1:67-80

A s much as we hate to admit, Christmastime can be a season of broken promises. The gifts that promise to fill us with joy and ease in December are forgotten or thrown away by January. The same seasonal events that once brought us emotional warmth and comfort now feel cold and distant. Advent gives us the space to wrestle and wonder: is there anyone or anything that makes good on its promises?

When Zechariah's gets his voice back from the Lord, he wants everyone to know that God always fulfills his promises. Like Mary, Zechariah responds to God's gracious work in song. Like his wife Elizabeth, Zechariah is filled with the Holy Spirit and prophesies.

Luke tells us that Zechariah's first words after his mouth was opened were to bless God,[1] so it should not surprise us to find that theme at the very beginning of his song. He knows that the only right response to the work of God to bring about the salvation of his people is to bless God's name in worship. When Zechariah praises God for this salvation, he uses the particular phrase, "horn of salvation." Interestingly, these same words appear in two other places in Scripture with striking connections.

---

1   Luke 1:64

The first place is in the poetic prayer of a woman named Hannah, who responds in praise to God after he opens her womb and gives her a child after years of barrenness, much like Elizabeth. She says,

> " 'My heart exults in the Lord;
>   my horn is exalted in the Lord.
> My mouth derides my enemies,
>   because I rejoice in your salvation.
> There is none holy like the Lord;
>   for there is none besides you;
>   there is no rock like our God.' "[2]

The second place is a song of King David found in Psalm 18.[3] There, David praises God for delivering him from the hand of all of his enemies and specifically from Saul. God sent Samuel to anoint him as king when he was still a boy, but he endured many years of struggle, hardship, and persecution. Here, many years later, David pens this lengthy psalm of praise to God. He attributes the peace and success of his kingdom not to himself, but to the Lord, saying,

> "The Lord is my rock and my fortress and my deliverer,
>   my God, my rock, in whom I take refuge,"
> "the word of the Lord proves true;
>   he is a shield for all those who take refuge in him."
> "Great salvation he brings to his king,
>   and shows steadfast love to his anointed,
>   to David and his offspring forever."[4]

Zechariah uses these same Spirit-inspired truths to craft his song of praise to God. He points to God's mercy and

---

2   1 Samuel 2:1-2
3   Specifically, Psalm 18:2, also quoted in 2 Samuel 22:3
4   Psalm 18:2, 30, 50

faithfulness to remember his promises and save his people. Just like King David had ushered in a time of peace after facing many foes, Zechariah believed that King Jesus was about to do the same.

Reaching further back, even beyond David, Zechariah praises God for remembering his promises to Abraham. God promised Abraham all the way back in the book of Genesis that he would be his shield and refuge and would make him into a great nation that would bless the nations.[5] This covenantal promise came with the sign of circumcision. No doubt Zechariah was recalling this promise in particular as he sang this song of praise on the day that his son John was circumcised.

In sum, Zechariah draws on all of this rich history to sing a song of how God is working in his lifetime to fulfill the promise to save his people.

When we come to faith in Christ, our lives take the same shape as this song. Without God's divine help, we are lost and without hope, but Jesus guarantees our salvation. As Paul writes in Ephesians 2, before Jesus, "you were dead in the trespasses and sins in which you once walked. But God, being rich in mercy, because of the great love with which he loved us, made us alive together with Christ—by grace you have been saved."[6] Even if you have been faithless in all of your promises, turn to our faithful God who promises to save you through faith.

Like Mary and Zechariah both, when we are given spiritual life, our first words should be praise to the Life-Giver. Not only our words, but also our works. "For we are his workmanship, created in Christ Jesus for good works."[7] Our lives should resound like a song of praise shown in obedience to the one who saved us.

Zechariah's song is the last we see or hear from him in Luke's account. Christian, are you leaving the same legacy? Will

---

5   Genesis 12:1-3, 15:1, 17:1-14

6   Ephesians 2:1-2a, 4-5

7   Ephesians 2:10

others remember you for having praised God and trusted in his promises? Over the centuries, we have a rich history in the men and women of faith who have gone before us. Take time this Advent to let their legacy of praise in writings, sermons, songs, and more compel you to worship the same Christ. In the midst of a world burdened by broken promises, let your life be a song of praise to the God whose promises never fail.

—— Day 15 ——

On the Horizon
Part III

So when the Lord calls you out to proclaim
The name of the One who will save
I pray that you will obey

MATTHEW 28:16-20

When Zechariah is moved to praise God in response to John's birth and circumcision, he begins by blessing God for his mighty work of raising up his king, his horn of salvation for the people of Israel, but he ends with a prophecy concerning his son John. He addresses John using a form of the same word Mary uses to refer to Israel as God's "servant." Just as Israel was called to be God's servant son, so Zechariah calls his son to become the same.

My own son is due to be born in several weeks from when I'm currently writing. I find myself filled with questions about all kinds of things. Will his hair be curly like mine or straight like his mom's? Will he be extroverted or introverted? Artsy or athletic? Tall or short? In the midst of these myriad questions, Zechariah addresses the most important one: Will my child be a servant of God?

Zechariah knows that his son will be uniquely filled with the Holy Spirit to accomplish a particular purpose, for that is the message he received from the angel Gabriel. Luke will go on to record, John will prepare the people of Israel for the coming Messiah by preaching repentance and forgiveness of sins, living out this calling faithfully.

John holds an extraordinary place in human history as the last prophet in the Old Testament pattern. He is the spiritual

Elijah promised in Malachi, the one who prepares the way for the Lord himself to come in the person of Jesus.[1] Though imperfect and at times filled with doubt, he declares the truth of God and points to Jesus as the world's only hope, baptizing those whom he calls to repent. John, called "the Baptist" for this, spends his life preaching the truth about the coming Messiah even to the point of death.

John's specific calling is historically unique. Jesus himself says in Matthew 11:11 that "among those born of women there has arisen no one greater than John the Baptist," but his next sentence is striking. He says, "yet the one who is least in the kingdom of heaven is greater than he." Perhaps John's ministry is more applicable to Christ's church today than we might think!

Zechariah was not introducing a new word of prophecy in his song of praise. He knew from Mary's visit and Elizabeth's prophetic declaration that God's Messiah was coming to the earth. If you compare Luke 1:76-79 to what Gabriel announces to Zechariah earlier in Luke 1:16-17, you can see that Zechariah is simply restating what God has already revealed to him. After calling John a prophet of the Most High, he outlines four tasks his ministry will fulfill. John will 1) go to prepare God's ways, 2) give knowledge of God's salvation, 3) shine upon those sitting in darkness, and 4) guide God's people into peace.

Each of these tasks point to the salvation which God provides through the cross and resurrection of Jesus. Jesus himself commissions his followers to complete four very similar tasks in Matthew 28:19-20: 1) go into all the world, 2) make disciples of all nations, 3) baptize them in his name, and 4) teach them to obey all his commands.

Have we not been commissioned to follow in John's footsteps by pointing others to Jesus? Zechariah's prophetic words

---

1   Malachi 4:5-6

should not simply remind us of John the Baptist's ministry. They need to resound in our hearts and minds as we consider the calling God has laid upon our lives. Like John, we have also been called to go with the gospel, teach with the gospel, illuminate with the gospel, and guide with the gospel.

There is no question about it: the sunrise that gives light to those who sit in darkness has been revealed in the life, death, and resurrection of Jesus. This is our only hope for salvation in this world. The Creator of all life has sent his son to redeem those who repent of their sins and believe in his name. Do you believe this?

If so, these are the questions that remain: will you reflect this light? Will you share the hope of the one who has saved you? Will you go into your corner of the world and speak of the one who has come? Consider who might see the light of Jesus this Christmas because of your faithfulness as a servant of God.

In the Days of Caesar
Part I

For the one who knows all men, Jesus is born

LUKE 2:1-7

The king we meet in the second chapter of Luke was no surprise to the reader. He came from a humble yet distinguished lineage of military leaders. His name literally meant "great" and his rule was majestic, ushering in a time of peace. This king, of course...was Caesar Augustus.

You may have been surprised just then, but Luke's audience was not. The Roman people in Luke's time were big fans of the kingdom their emperor had created. The elite were wealthy, successful, peaceful, and prosperous because of their leaders, and to them, society only seemed to be getting better.

As seemingly random as Caesar Augustus is to us, so Luke's mention of his census seems strangely random in the context of this story. What is so important about this census?

The work of registering people by census has been in use for thousands of years. In almost every instance, its purpose is to acquire information that will build up the kingdom of its ruler. We see this happen throughout Scripture. In Exodus 30, God commanded his people Israel to take a census in order to provide for the priests and the tabernacle. This work was done so that atonement for sins by sacrifice could continue to be made by the priests on behalf of the people. Later on in Israel's history, in 1 Chronicles 21, King David sinfully required a census to be taken of Israel, not for the sake of sacrifice and worship, but for the sake of assessing his military might. Here in Luke 2, the pagan Caesar Augustus registered his own kingdom for the sake of taxation. This money supported various infrastructures and built up his own house.

But above all of this, the author of Psalm 87 reminds us that God is the true ruler and registrar of his people. Speaking of God's eternal kingdom, he says, "and of Zion it shall be said, 'This one and that one were born in her'; for the Most High himself will establish her. The LORD records as he registers the peoples, 'This one was born there.'"[1]

God does not simply know his people intimately because of his supreme intelligence to count them, but because of his divine omnipotence to *create* them. When the governor Quirinius requires the people of his locality to register at their ancestral homes, he's just cataloguing their place of birth for tax purposes. But when God registers his people, he doesn't just know their place of birth—he causes them to be born.

We may selfishly seek to be served through wish lists and holiday plans. We may greedily chase after our own gain through working overtime. We might even obsessively control others' affections through the things we buy and give. All of these efforts prove how much our flesh desires to assess and build up our own kingdoms. But Jesus, the Savior who made us, came "not to be served, but to serve, and to give his life as a ransom for many."[2] He even taught the people to pay taxes to the government that would unjustly murder him, knowing that his legally unjust death would be the vehicle of divine justice for our salvation.[3]

The prophetic birth of this Jesus in King David's hometown came about when two humble citizens simply obeyed the census of Caesar Augustus. That is the sovereign power that God alone has over human history.

As believers of the good news of Jesus Christ, we have been adopted into an eternal family and given a new and

---

1   Psalm 87:5-6
2   Mark 10:35
3   Luke 20:19-26

lasting birthright. God foreknew this in his own census taken long before any of us were ever born.[4] That's why we can have confidence in his kingdom while living in the midst of broken ones. God's word and gospel is a sure foundation of hope and direction for those living in a broken and hopeless world because he creates, knows, saves, and sustains us.

This hope does not come from the temporary peace made by politicians, and God's call to humbly submit to imperfect authorities is not an endorsement of them. No, our hope is in Jesus, the only eternal king. Turn from all lesser hopes and trust in him, knowing that when you do, God has your name written down in his book of life to be remembered for all eternity.[5]

Jesus may have lived briefly as a citizen of Caesar's kingdom but he came to establish God's eternal kingdom. The kingdom of Caesar Augustus has long lay in ruin, with most of its citizens completely forgotten, but the kingdom of Jesus Christ is still very much alive, recruiting a divine list of global citizens across all human history. And one day, the book of that census will be opened, and not a single name who has believed in him will be forgotten.

---

4   Ephesians 1:3-10
5   Luke 10:20, Revelation 21:27

— Day 17 —

In the Days of Caesar
Part II

For the promised prince of old, Jesus is born

PHILIPPIANS 2:5-11

As we saw on Days 7 and 8, the Bible speaks very little of Joseph, the adoptive father of Jesus. When Luke introduces him back in Luke 1:27 as Mary's betrothed, he describes him this way: "a man whose name was Joseph." Wow. How illustrious.

Luke 2:4-5 at least gives us some more detail. It says that Joseph went up to his hometown to be registered in Bethlehem at the behest of the Roman government. We have, at this point, about the same information on Joseph as someone on a social media "Suggested Friends" list.

But the author does include a critical detail that helps us see the bigger picture. In both passages which mention Joseph, Luke lets us know that he is from the house of David. This is a crucial reference for the knowledgable Israelite reader. Almost a thousand years before Joseph, God established the shepherd warrior David as king over his people. Anointed by prophet and affirmed by victory, David rose to power through patient obedience to God during King Saul's cruel reign. He sought to honor God by building a house for his presence to dwell where his people could worship, but God responded with a gracious rebuttal and an astounding promise: "The Lord declares to you that the Lord will make you a house. When your days are fulfilled and you lie down with your fathers, I will raise up your offspring after you, who shall come from your body, and I will establish his kingdom. He shall build a house for my name, and I will establish the throne of his kingdom forever. And your house and your kingdom shall be made sure forever before me. Your throne shall be established forever."[1]

God's shocking reversal of David's wish displays God's kindness and grace at work in the world. God stepped into the darkness of the world and set up a light for the nations, a leader whose descendent would one day reign forever. Luke wants us to understand that Joseph's pilgrimage to Bethlehem was far from simple civil obedience. It was the very act of God to fulfill this kingly prophecy. As we saw back on Day 1, the prophet Micah picks up on this same promise in a prophecy about David's hometown of Bethlehem. He says, "But you, O Bethlehem Ephrathah, who are too little to be among the clans of Judah, from you shall come forth for me one who is to be ruler in Israel, whose coming forth is from of old, from ancient days."[2]

When we celebrate the birth of Jesus, we are right to celebrate him as king and lord. Just think of how many Christmas songs declare Jesus as king.

"Angels From the Realms of Glory" — *Worship Christ the newborn king...*
"Silent Night" — *Jesus, Lord at thy birth...*
"What Child is This" - *This, this is Christ the king...*
"Hark! the Herald Angels Sing" — *Glory to the newborn king...*
"The First Noel" — *Born is the King of Israel...*

And there are still others. But remember, despite the kingly promise God made in ages past, Joseph lived no kingly life. Much like his son would do, Joseph spent his earthly days in humility, far from palace, position, and power. God used his humble obedience as a servant to bring about the birth of his promised king.

---

1   2 Samuel 7:11b-12 & 16
2   Micah 5:2

As we read in Philippians 2, Jesus himself also walked in humble obedience as a servant. In an even greater way than his father, Jesus emptied himself of earthly comfort and honor, even to the point of death on a cross, so that we who believe in him might be saved.

Let this be an encouragement to us when our lives, much less our Christmas plans, feel pretty unremarkable. Rather than trying to dress them up with thrill, excitement, and intrigue, what if we leaned into the tedium and walked by faith? If the life of Joseph and his adopted son Jesus is any indication, God can do infinitely more with an average person living an average life by faith than he can with a remarkable public figure living out a thrilling schedule. If you are a Christian, you obtained an even better heritage than Joseph when you believed in Jesus. You are not just the descendent of an ancient king—you are co-heirs with the reigning King himself.

The humble obedience of Jesus was not only the pathway to our salvation, but his own exaltation. The season of Advent should remind us that our king will one day return, and he will not be concerned with our earthly titles and our recognition before men. Only our humble testimony of his kingly work will remain. Let us spend this season, then, magnifying the name of our king through a humble faith.

— Day 18 —

ɪn the Days of Caesar
Part III

For the Christ the son of God, Jesus is born

ISAIAH 53

To this day, my favorite Christmas decoration to put up is our Christmas tree. Our family falls firmly on the "real" side of the debate between real and plastic trees. We prefer the messy branches, needles, and pine scent over the convenience and reusability. Even in our small apartment, we still choose to prioritize this annual tradition by temporarily replacing one of our living room chairs with a six-foot noble fir. No question about it.

Of course, these and other Christmas trappings were not a part of Joseph and Mary's culture. In fact, besides Caesar's census, Luke makes no mention of any particular festival or holiday when Joseph and Mary traveled to Bethlehem. As would be expected in that day, Joseph and Mary would have stayed with a local family, likely Joseph's own. While staying there, Luke tells us that Mary went into labor and gave birth to Jesus—God's own son in the flesh, the savior of the world, the eternal king of promise.

Luke describes his birth without fanfare. In fact, he ends his simple description of the birth of Jesus with an odd and humiliating detail. He tells us that after he was born, his mom "wrapped him in swaddling cloths and laid him in a manger, because there was no place for them in the inn."[1]

You may notice, this detail doesn't exactly match our popularized depictions of the birth of Christ. Apparently,

---

1   Luke 2:7

there was no frenzied, late-night search for an open room at an inn. I use the word "inn" (the ESV's translation) in the song lyrics, but the Greek word translated as "inn" here is translated as "guest room" elsewhere in Scripture.

Regardless, Joseph and Mary had already been in Bethlehem for some amount of time, so the circumstances are still humiliating. Why did no one make room for poor Mary? Why did God allow his own son to be born in this way?

When we compare the bookending verses of Luke 2:1-7, the description stands out even more. Luke begins by telling us that the king in power sent out a decree for "all the world" to be registered, and his decree was carried out dutifully. His officials carried it out so effectively that Joseph, even though his wife was approaching her due date, took a journey across the country in order to obey it. Then, Luke ends the passage by telling us that the king of all the world, after being born to a young virgin from a small town, was laid in an animal trough because there was no other room for him.

My wife and I make annual room for our Christmas tree because we love it. The world made no room for its savior because it did not love him. How could we? We didn't even know him yet, and even if we had, our sinful hearts would not have loved him. "But God shows his love for us in that while we were still sinners, Christ died for us."[2] Thankfully, the one least lovely to us has become our source of greatest joy.

This is who Jesus was prophesied to be. "He was despised and rejected by men; a man of sorrows, and acquainted with grief; and as one from whom men hide their faces he was despised, and we esteemed him not."[3] The prophet Isaiah goes on to say that though we all have gone astray from God our shepherd, he made himself to be a sheep who bore our iniquity and died so that we might live. All who would receive

---

2   Romans 5:8
3   Isaiah 53:3

this life must turn from lesser Caesars and surrender themselves by faith to him.

This Advent, prepare your heart to make room for Christ. Read Scripture and books, sing songs and carols, and take part in activities that cause you to focus on Jesus. Pray, worship, meditate, and focus your minds and hearts…but remember that before all of these wonderful things, Jesus first made room in you.

If it were up to us alone to make room for Jesus, we would have lost all hope, but God has made his own way into our inhospitable world, into our own lack of regard and preparation. At the cross, he transformed the greatest humiliation into our sure salvation. It is to our benefit that Jesus entered in at the lowest place so that we who are lowly might be lifted up in him, and so that we who did not seek him out would find him as he comes to us.

This is the hope that Luke records in the humble manger.

The king of promise was born, and since no one in town would show him esteem or regard, God would call out his worshipers from the surrounding fields.

—— Day 19 ——

When the Shepherds
Kept Their Watching
Part I

And while Bethlehem was sleeping, there were angels aloft
Not over palaces or temples, but over shepherds and flocks

LUKE 2:8-14

"When the shepherds kept their watching, there were no silent flocks. There were animals bleating at simple men at their jobs." So reads the opening lines of the first draft of this song.

My pastor and friends rightly suggested that I should change the word "bleating" to something else—"calling" in the final version—because the word sounds awkward and could be confused with "bleeding." It was a helpful lyrical edit, and definitely the right call. But after further study, I wonder if there is something truer to the text in that original wording.

There are countless other devotionals, books, and sermons which highlight the decrepit state of shepherds in that ancient culture, but the point is still important for us to consider every Advent. Shepherds make frequent appearance throughout biblical history, however familiar they are to us.

Of course, we're familiar with the *idea* of shepherds—the quaint, pastoral, Christmastime nativity figurine of a young boy with a sweet lamb draped across his shoulders, which is so far removed from the actual thing. Visit any farm for any amount of time and you'll encounter the real picture: dirty wool, biting flies, smelly dung, broken limbs, noisy herds, and messy births.

The first shepherd in the Bible, Abel, was murdered in anger and jealousy by his brother Cain. Isaac's deceptive father-in-law, Laban, was a shepherd along with his daughter Rachel. Isaac's son Jacob followed in the same path, and as a result, his family was asked to live outside of town in Egypt. Moses's father-in-law was a shepherd, too, and it was while he was in his employ that God chose to reveal himself and begin his plan of redeeming his people. As a boy, David was a shepherd when he was anointed as king, rose up to defeat Goliath, and then went into the wilderness to escape death by Saul's hand. It seems as though each time shepherds are mentioned, God is at work calling worshipers out from the lowest of places.[1]

For as many shepherds as appear throughout the Bible, though, there is one whom we are quick to forget: God himself. In fact, more than a third of the references to shepherds in the Bible speak of the character of God toward his people. From Genesis 49:24 to Revelation 7:17, God reveals himself as the one who carries and leads his people to green pasture. He guides them with his skillful hand and provides for their every need. However you may see this image depicted, the analogy is not meant to paint God as clean or quaint. The God who shepherds is a God of immense patience, surprising humility, and discerning authority. He is gracious and compassionate, gentle and lowly, willing to stoop down and work in our dust and dung to give life to the creatures he loves.

When the angels come down to deliver the good news of Jesus's birth to the Bethlehem shepherds, it flew in the face of the purpose of Caesar's decree. His top-down registration is inverted in this bottom-up declaration of God's salvation. This "good news of great joy that will be for *all* the people" started with those lowly shepherds.

---

1   Genesis 4:2, 29:9, 46:34; Exodus 3:1; 1 Samuel 16:11

Don't miss the significance in verse 12, when the angels tell the shepherds, "this will be a sign for you." The arms-wide-open welcome of this good news from God becomes close and personal with those two simple words: "*for you.*" We would do well to consider their implication.

When God brings the good news of the birth of his own Son, the hero of Israel and bringer of salvation, he doesn't announce it loudly at the Jerusalem Temple, nor from Herod's palace or any other earthly throne. He brings it humbly and personally to a group of shepherds.

Friend, he has come down for *you.* Do you know him? Not just about him in books and sermons or wishful thoughts and stories at a distance—do you know him like a sheep knows its shepherd? God has made himself known to you in Christ, and he calls you to put your faith in him.

The baby announced to the shepherds would grow up to teach them, "I am the good shepherd. I know my own and my own know me."[2] Know Jesus by faith, and find life in him. Trust Jesus by faith, and walk with him, even when he leads you through dark valleys. Find rest in his loving, saving work, and follow him all the days of your life.

---

2   John 10:14

When the Shepherds
Kept Their Watching
Part II

Glory to God!
Glory in the highest!

PSALM 24

You may be shocked to learn, as I was, that according to Luke's account, the angels in this story do not sing. The Bible is never explicitly clear that angels sing at all, but simply that they praise God by giving glory to him. In fact, even though I have spoken previously of Mary's and Zechariah's songs, the Bible is not even clear if *they* sang.

Here in Luke 2, the heavenly host of angels is recorded as praising God in saying, "Glory to God in the highest, and on earth peace among those with whom he is pleased!" Luke's implication is that this group of messengers from heaven looks and sounds more like an invading army than like a choir concert.

Don't get me wrong: I *love* choirs. I adore music, and especially at Christmas. I worked more meticulously on the choral section of this particular song than any other part of the album. I would even contend that the angels likely did and do sing in heaven, based on other descriptions in Scripture, but the musicality of their delivery is not the point. The point, according to Luke, is what they're actually saying: "glory to God!"

In Psalm 24, David calls God the king of glory, "the Lord strong and mighty, the Lord mighty in battle."[1] He paints us

---

1   Psalm 24:8

a picture of a great warrior king whose mighty character and pure merit grants him entrance into the grandest city and the holiest palace of heaven. He is a king worthy of worship, adoration, fear, submission, and honor.

This is the king announced by the angels. God's glory is "in the highest" because he is the King Most High. There are no other gods higher than or beside him, no other powers or entities who can compare to his glory. He made the world and everything in it, and we understand him by the regular expression of his immutable attributes of power, wisdom, love, and holiness throughout Scripture. His Spirit, who moved in the life of his people in the past, still moves today. He gives life through faith to dead hearts, spiritual insight through preaching to open minds, and power through prayer to those walking in faith.

Jesus, being the Son of the Most High, shares in this glory. There is no greater king, god, ruler, leader, or hero than Jesus Christ. Even at the lowest and most humble moments of his life, the glory of God was manifested perfectly in Jesus. We certainly see it here at his birth in the praise of the heavenly host, but we also see it clearly at his baptism, transfiguration, and even at his death on the cross, where the Roman exclaimed, "surely this is the Son of God!"[2]

In sum, as the apostle John describes, "the Word became flesh and dwelt among us, and we have seen his glory, glory as of the only Son from the Father, full of grace and truth."[3] This is the glory that the angels declare in the heavens above the shepherds in Luke 2:14.

The angels' declaration ends with the Greek word *eudokia*, which the ESV translates as a five-word phrase: "with whom he is pleased." The idea here is that of God's delight and benevolence, his kindness that revealed by grace rather than earned or obtained by merit.

---

2   Luke 3:21-22, 9:28-36, & 23:47
3   John 1:14

Jesus is later recorded as using the same word in Luke 10:21 when he speaks about the truth of the gospel. There, after speaking about the precious gift of salvation given to his followers, he prays, "I thank you, Father, Lord of heaven and earth, that you have hidden these things from the wise and understanding and revealed them to little children; yes, Father, for such was your gracious *will*," or delight, or pleasure. Jesus echoes the same worshipful announcement of the angels when he affirms that God's pleasure comes not to those who earn it, but to those who receive it as a gift.

This Christmas season, remember that the salvation offered in Christ alone is truly a gift. If God's glory reigns supreme over the entire universe, no amount of effort could earn, obtain, or match it. God shows his glory when he reconciles with the ones who have rebelled against him. If you desire God's glory, be reconciled to God in Christ. Turn to him in faith and receive the gift he has promised.

When we come to faith in Christ, the glory of God springs to life in our hearts like the first hearthfire of the season. Throughout our lives, that fire grows and shines through our faith, obedience, perseverance through suffering, transformation into his likeness, and declaration of his gospel. In all these things, God calls us to glorify him in this world. This is the purpose for which we were made!

Whether we sing it, say it, or show it, our lives should declare with the psalmist: "Not to us, O Lord, not to us, but to your name give glory, for the sake of your steadfast love and your faithfulness!"[4] Indeed, "he is the King of glory!"[5]

---

4   Psalm 115:1
5   Psalm 24:10

Let Us Go
Part I

To think that God would come to us so humbly
To think he'd save ones who were so undeserving

LUKE 2:13-20, 1 JOHN 1:1-4

For as long as Christmas has been celebrated, the idea of peace has been a prevalent theme. You can find it in the songs of the season, the sentiments of advertisements, and the seasonal goals of various organizations. When engaged with genuinely, much good can be accomplished. The hungry are fed, the poor are provided for, and all kinds of humanitarian efforts are made to increase the quality of life. Peace on earth, so to speak.

These are good and wonderful things, but they beg the question: what is the goal of peace, and how do we obtain it? Is there an end to the needs which cause death when unmet? Is there a cure for all diseases, or a treaty for all disunity?

The Holy Spirit speaking through the prophet Isaiah makes a bold claim about the one who governs peace in Isaiah 9:6. He says,

> "For to us a child is born,
>   to us a son is given;
> and the government shall be upon his shoulder,
>   and his name shall be called
> Wonderful Counselor, Mighty God,
>   Everlasting Father, Prince of Peace."

In Luke 2, when the angels proclaimed that peace had come among those with whom God is pleased, they told the shepherds to go and see a newborn child. Having just talked about a government census, Luke is cueing his readers in to the mysterious work of God to bring his Prince of Peace to the earth. What peace did the shepherds find when they went to see the child?

As we considered in yesterday's devotional, these shepherds were among the very first people to see God in the flesh and behold his glory. They can say, quite literally, in the words of 1 John 1:1-2, "That which was from the beginning, which we have heard, which we have seen with our eyes, which we looked upon and have touched with our hands, concerning the word of life—the life was made manifest, and we have seen it." What a gift to be able to see the newborn Jesus lying in the manger! Many of us would jump at the opportunity now to do the same, but Jesus has powerful words for those who have not seen him in the flesh.

After he died on the cross and rose from the grave, he appeared to many of his disciples to prove himself alive to them, but his disciple Thomas had yet to see him. The apostle John records that Thomas doubted, so Jesus graciously revealed himself to him in the flesh and said, "'Put your finger here, and see my hands; and put out your hand, and place it in my side. Do not disbelieve, but believe.' Thomas answered him, 'My Lord and my God!' Jesus said to him, 'Have you believed because you have seen me? Blessed are those who have not seen and yet have believed.'"[1] John concludes by saying, "Now Jesus did many other signs in the presence of the disciples, which are not written in this book; but these are written so that you may believe that Jesus is the Christ, the Son of God, and that by believing you may have life in his name."

Thus, the first application of the shepherd's story is not to seek peace in personal efforts or experiences, but to believe in Jesus and find life in him. This is the true peace of heaven.

---

1   John 20:27-31

Do you feel the weight of unrest in our world today? Do you feel powerless to help, too far removed from everything that is good? Jesus can empathize. He stepped into this broken world and lived a life full of unrest, but he laid it down on the cross to conquer death for you, because he loves you. There is nothing you have done or can ever do that would disqualify you from the peace that he offers through faith. He delights to give it to you as a gift, just as he welcomed outcast shepherds and doubting Thomas. See his saving work, put your faith in him, and find true and everlasting peace.

The second application stems directly from this, because when you believe in Jesus like the shepherds, you become a testimony of his peace to others. We already looked at 1 John 1:1-2 above. Immediately after, John writes, "And [we] testify to it and proclaim to you the eternal life, which was with the Father and was made manifest to us—that which we have seen and heard we proclaim also to you, so that you too may have fellowship with us; and indeed our fellowship is with the Father and with his Son Jesus Christ."

The goal of God's peace is a thriving fellowship with God himself that should compel us to live in community with his people and declare his gospel in his world.

I am so grateful to have had the chance to record this Christmas album, and my prayer is that it will herald the good news of Jesus to all who are willing to listen. But this Christmas, the greatest testimony of God's peace for those around you is not this album nor any other work of art you may encounter or enjoy this season.

Christian, it's *you*. It's Christ working through his Spirit in you and your local church. The shepherds went to find the Prince of Peace lying in a manger and then declared it to all who would hear. Christian, Let your words and actions be like a declaration of this peace to a weary world, a song of good news that brings great joy to those who believe its message.

Let Us Go
Part II

We can't contain this love
It's for the world to see

LUKE 10:1-20

I have always loved seeing nativity scenes at Christmas. There's a certain wonder in the arrangement of all of these characters with their faces gazing at the Christ child, with the humility of the shepherd boy, the majesty of the kings, the humanity of the baby lying in hay, and the glory of the angel looking down from above.

Of course, all of our nativity scenes have little inaccuracies. The figurines look more like pageant characters than first-century Palestinians. According to Matthew, the Magi aren't described as kings and they were never at the manger. According to our story in Luke, multiple angels appeared to the shepherds out in the fields, but not at the manger.

Nevertheless, the central story of that scene is absolutely true, and it reveals a powerful message. Notice how it develops in Luke 2:8-20. First, an angel of the Lord appears to the shepherds to announce the coming of God's Savior and Christ in Bethlehem. Then, a host of angels appears alongside that messenger in full agreement, praising God and magnifying his glory through this message. Afterward, the shepherds go and see the promised newborn child wrapped in swaddling clothes and lying in a manger. Upon seeing him, they go and make this good news known to others, going out to praise God together "for all they had heard and seen."[1]

---

1   Luke 2:20

This story is, in effect, the Bible in miniature. It takes the major elements of the whole narrative of Scripture. As in the Old Testament, Jesus is anticipated in the announcement of the angels. As in the Gospels, Jesus is manifested in the promised child lying in a manger. As in Acts and the letters of the New Testament, Jesus is proclaimed out in the world by the shepherds and pondered by Mary in her heart.

Remember how the angels announced peace on earth between God and man? Interestingly, when Jesus sends out his followers in Luke 10, he also instructs them to announce peace to those they come across in hopes of finding "sons of peace" and to preach to them that "the kingdom of God has come."[2] When they declare this good news, Jesus knows that not everyone will accept it. In fact, Jesus has strong words of judgment toward those who refuse it, likening their eventual destruction to that of Sodom in Genesis, an unrepentant city consumed by fire.

This is not a scene we would want depicted with painted figurines, but it is an important reminder for us. The good news of God's peace is good because of how desperately we need it. Our brokenness because of sin leaves us in just condemnation before God. Without faith in Christ, we await the same fate as those who refused to believe in Christ's kingdom then. Though Jesus came as a baby to bring peace, he promises to return in power to establish the full peace of his kingdom through the destruction of the wicked and the punishment of hell. The promise of his eternal justice is a warning to the unrepentant, but it is the hope of all who believe.

That's why the shepherds responded with such exuberant joy. They went out to declare that true peace from heaven was now available to the world because they knew Jesus, God's Savior, had been born into the world. Through faith, the shepherds' hope is also our hope, and even more so because

2   Luke 10:5 & 9

of the death and resurrection of Jesus, the whole scope of his gospel.

Christian, this Christmas has afforded you ample opportunities to herald that same good news. Our goal is not to make sales pitches or trick unwitting pageant attendees into uncomfortable situations, but to magnify the glory of Jesus by responding to his coming in the same way that the shepherds did. And our message, like theirs, is for those whom the world has pushed aside or forgotten about, those who realize their desperate need for heavenly peace.

The shepherds were the first to hear of this good news, but they were far from the last. In Luke's sequel, the book of Acts, he records how the gospel spread through Jerusalem and beyond, reaching not just Jews but people from all nations. That's why the apostle Paul made it his aim "to preach the gospel, not where Christ has already been named, lest [he] build on someone else's foundation, but as it is written, 'Those who have never been told of him will see, and those who have never heard will understand.'"[3] Just like the shepherds, Paul saw the glory of God in Jesus Christ, believed in him, received his peace, and made it his mission to declare it to the world.

Don't miss the story for the scene! Don't let your local observance of this season limit the scope of your prayers, gifts, and efforts. Consider how the nations could hear of the good news of Jesus through how you and your family celebrate this Advent and Christmas. Go to the ones who are far and share the hope that you have found in Jesus, the good news of his salvation.

As I set up my own nativity at home and enjoy seeing the ones on display around town, I want to remember the true message of that scene. The same figurines still stand on my shelf every year, but the people they represent are long gone. God dispersed them all soon after that worshipful moment,

---

3   Romans 15:20-21

sending them abroad to bring the good news of his kingdom to the nations. May God do also with me and with all who have seen this Jesus and believed, that we may give our lives to make this gospel known to the world.

— Day 23 —

The Coming King (Reprise)
Part I

Let us rise, wanderers in the night
Following his light
Now shining for the world to see

MATTHEW 2

A couple years into playing the early songs from *Good News, Great Joy* for my church, I starting getting several requests from church members and friends. "Are you going to write more songs?" "What about a song for Joseph?" "Ooh, you should write a song for the wisemen!"

Honestly, I was initially hesitant, but as I sat on the ideas more and more, I realized that there were already themes in Luke's gospel account that Matthew's account echoed regarding these same characters. I worked to write some of those songs, and three resulted from that effort: "Son of David," written from Joseph's perspective, and "The Coming King"/"The Coming King (Reprise)," written loosely from the Magi's. The latter serve as a sort of frame story perspective for the album, treating the Magi like outside narrators who introduce and conclude the whole album.

As we remembered yesterday, though we put these characters up as part of our nativity sets, they don't really belong in that same scene—but it is clear that the Magi were acquainted with the prophecies which pointed to that scene. They had read about how the God of Israel had promised a Messiah would come and rescue his people.

He would come as a prophet who would plant God's righteous truth in people's hearts. He would come as a priest who would take their iniquity and cleanse them in a day. He would come as a king who would save them from all of their enemies.[1]

In response to these prophecies, the Magi followed a miraculous star that lead them to Jerusalem, where King Herod ruled. Matthew's account of Christ's birth draws a stark distinction between the Magi and King Herod. Though a practicing Jew, Herod believed nothing about God's promised king to Israel except that he was a potential threat to his domination. The Magi, on the other hand, were foreigners who had such a great knowledge of the Scriptures that they understood the prophecy of Israel's Messiah and journeyed in faith to find him.

It didn't take long for each side to prove their true hearts. The Magi worshiped Jesus and brought him gifts. Herod sent soldiers to quell the threat to his rule and murdered the children of Bethlehem.

Our world has plenty of Herods. Most of us will face similar challenges as the Magi, which require boldness in truth, a perseverance in opposition, and wisdom that leads to worship. However, we should quickly seek out the Herods hiding in our own hearts, for we have all lived like him. We have treated the Christ of Christmas like a thing to be exploited rather than a king to be worshiped and obeyed. We have traded the wondrous news of his coming for cheap sales pitches and pithy aphorisms. We have fought wars on culture and tradition rather than serving our communities and preaching the gospel of Jesus.

As Advent draws quickly to its close and Christmas Day draws near, consider your posture toward Jesus. Will you spend your time in worship or selfishness? Will your life be marked by a growing understanding of Jesus that leads to worship, or

---

1   Deuteronomy 18:15, Jeremiah 31:33, Zechariah 13:1, Psalm 2:1-12

a growing self-reliance that denies his rule? Confess your sin and submit to Christ's true kingship.

Then, worship him like the Magi! They give us such a wonderful reminder of what a heart of wonder-filled worship and obedience to Christ looks like. In fact, Matthew records their response to the star that led them to Christ with a phrase that should be familiar to us: "When they saw the star, they rejoiced exceedingly with *great joy*."[2]

Much like the shepherds, the revelation of God through his word and the miraculous sight in the heavens drew the Magi near to see God's glory. They responded with great joy to the star because they had an understanding of its good news. The tidings of that miraculous sight brought them right up to face of God in the incarnate Christ so that they might worship him. The great joy which filled their hearts overflowed into their gifts of worship.

Our efforts to serve our neighbors and the watching world with the love of Christ may seem less remarkable than that star, but they are no less brilliant. Yes, our world has world has plenty of Heroes, but it is also filled with men and women like the Magi. They have heard of God's goodness and mighty works, and he is making their hearts ready for faith in him. Let us with ever-growing grace and truth declare that Jesus Christ, born in Bethlehem, lived, died, and rose again so that every weary traveler who comes to him by faith may worship him as their everlasting king.

---

2   Matthew 2:10

The Coming King (Reprise)
Part II

Behold! Immanuel will come

ACTS 1:6-11

For the last several years, I have spent every Christmas Eve night playing through the songs of *Good News, Great Joy* for my home church. Though our production is simple—mostly acoustic guitars accompanying a few voices—the performance is hard work. I know most musicians and worship pastors can relate, as the Christmas season almost always involves our most extensive and exhausting work of the year. As such, I end each Advent season feeling tired yet full of the season's longing. This has become a dear tradition for me and our church. Right as the last hours of Advent come to a close, the vivid reminder of Christ's coming brings the season's real purpose back into focus.

We have now spent many days unpacking the beauty of Christ's coming, which is the focus of Luke's first two chapters. The promised king was born so long ago, but the annual rehearsal of his coming is so good for every believer to observe, both by anticipation during Advent and celebration at Christmas. When we remember his first coming, we remember God's faithfulness to save his people, the good news which has brought us great joy through faith in Christ. The rest of Luke's gospel account records how Jesus embodies and accomplishes the sure hope of this good news in his perfect life, sacrificial death, and glorious resurrection—and then Luke ends his book with this brief story:

"While [Jesus] blessed [his disciples], he parted from them and was carried up into heaven. And they worshiped him and returned to Jerusalem with great joy, and were continually in the temple blessing God."[1]

The disciples, like the shepherds, respond to Jesus with great joy and go out into the world to tell others about him, just as we would expect. But at the end of the story, the king of promise vanishes.

This long-expected king of glory, the one whose coming Luke described in such great detail in the opening chapters of his gospel, this great king now quickly ascends to heaven without any fanfare at all. In a story about a king and a kingdom, why is the king suddenly gone?

Perhaps Theophilus had a similar question, because Luke wrote a sequel for him in the book of Acts, which opens with that same short scene told in greater detail. He writes that two angels appeared to the disciples as they stood dumfounded and looking skyward after Christ's ascension. They say, "'Men of Galilee, why do you stand looking into heaven? This Jesus, who was taken up from you into heaven, will come in the same way as you saw him go into heaven.'"[2]

If Jesus were to stay, we would presume that more teachings and work needed to be done, but because he left, we can trust his powerful words on the cross: "It is finished."[3] By leaving, Jesus declares his perfect work of salvation is truly complete, but he also punctuates the responsibility of his followers to accomplish his mission here on earth. His absence is the catalyst for the coming of His Spirit residing in every believer, every citizen in his kingdom. His ascension does not signal his evacuation from this world, but his invasion, which testifies to his heavenly reign. The rest of the book of Acts proves this as his church multiplies and fills the earth. But according to the

---

1   Luke 24:51-53
2   Acts 1:11
3   John 19:30

angels, the great hope in the ascension of Jesus is the promise of his eventual return.

This was not new information for the disciples, but as their friend and teacher Jesus ascended up into the clouds, they were distracted by thoughts of an earthly kingdom. They should have thought back to the last time they were distracted by similar thoughts, as recorded in Luke 19. During that moment, Jesus told them a parable about a king who traveled to receive a kingdom. Before leaving, he called servants and gave them money to invest until he returned. When he returned, he found that while some took their investment and multiplied it, one particular servant doubted the king's faithfulness and selfishly hid the money away. The king called him wicked, and took away even what he was given.[4]

Jesus wanted the disciples to make good investments with the hope that he had given, and he wants the same for us in this season. The true object of our longing every Advent should not be a backward wistfulness regarding the stories of Christ's birth or an earthly focus on temporary celebrations, but a forward expectation of Christ's glorious and imminent return.

The Bible teaches that when Jesus returns, he will make all things new. He will gather his people once and for all, and they will receive his glorious inheritance of a kingdom without pain, sickness, sin, or death.[5] But as he warned the disciples through the parable, the hope of his second coming demands a response. As the last hours of Advent come to a close, consider: do you believe in Christ's first coming? If so, do you really believe he is coming again? What is the status of his investment in you? Has your life been transformed such that it reflects his good news? Have you invested that good news into others?

---

4   Luke 19:11-27
5   Revelation 21:1-22:5

There are all kinds of concerts, pageants, and traditions that we can enjoy being a part of each Christmas season, but there's only one story capable of changing our hearts and transforming our lives: the gospel of Jesus Christ. Until he returns, what are you going to do with it?

For Christmas Day
(In the Days of Caesar — Part IV)

"For the one who comes by faith in Jesus is born"

JOHN 3:1-21

Through the long journey of Advent, we have finally come to the great celebration of Christmas Day. It is filled with some of life's sweetest memories, moments that you will no doubt experience this very day as you give and open gifts, eat cookies and holiday treats, and spend cherished time with loved ones. In the midst of these many wonderful things, take a moment to consider this day.

Today, we celebrate a savior who, while being God, was born of man.

If you've followed along with each devotional, you have encountered the Jesus who was born of the virgin Mary in Bethlehem. He is the promised Messiah for God's people, those who recognize their brokenness, repent of their sin, and put their faith in him. He is the promised king of God's kingdom, not just for ancient Israel but also for believers throughout the ages, from every nation on the planet.

Your days and weeks may have been leading up to this very day with great expectations, but remember: God interrupted human history with the birth of his son so that a people not expecting him would be saved. When you and your loved ones face unexpected trials, troubles, and disappointments this Christmas, remember that Jesus came humbly on an otherwise random day in a forgotten town to a lowly family. At the same time, when you and your loved ones open up intentional gifts and all of your plans go perfectly, remember that Jesus is the true gift of this and every season, the one who came to save you at precisely the right time and in the right way.

Today we celebrate a savior who, while being God, was born of man—but we can also celebrate those who, while being man, can be born of God.

This was his teaching to Nicodemus, a man of the Pharisees who came to Jesus by night to learn from him. As a teacher, Nicodemus had a good bit of knowledge about the promised Christ, but he had yet to follow God in faith. He thought he was going to meet with Jesus to learn more about God from him, but Jesus was about to reveal himself as God to him. In doing so, Jesus called Nicodemus out from simple knowledge *about* God into a saving and loving relationship *with* God.

Jesus told him, "'Truly, truly, I say to you, unless one is born again he cannot see the kingdom of God. For God so loved the world, that he gave his only Son, that whoever believes in him should not perish but have eternal life. For God did not send his Son into the world to condemn the world, but in order that the world might be saved through him. Whoever believes in him is not condemned, but whoever does not believe is condemned already, because he had not believed in the name of the only Son of God."[1]

Nicodemus did not remain in unbelief, but turned in faith to believe this good news which transformed him. He went from approaching Jesus timidly at night for information to following him boldly to his cross and helping bury his body in the tomb from which he would rise.[2]

We, likewise, cannot worship Christ for his birth without remembering his death and resurrection, which is the pinnacle of his saving work. The birth of Jesus is also the hope of our new birth in him, the spiritual birth that comes by grace through faith. When we understand God's gracious redemption

---

1   John 3:3, 16-18
2   John 19:39

in the coming of Christ, the only right response is to turn from sin and believe in him.

There is no day in your life, Christmas or otherwise, that Jesus does not want to redeem you for his kingdom and purpose. There is no situation or person that he will recoil from. The story of Christmas proves that Jesus draws near to show his great love for you. Remember that today's celebrations, as wonderful as they may be, are still a meager precursor to his glorious return. Align your heart to this reality and hold fast to the hope only found in him.

For those of us who have found this new birth in Jesus, let us praise him for it. May our lives be a witness to the manifold joys of Christ this Christmas. Let us fill today with worshipful celebration alike to the glorious excitement of the angels' praise and the humble sacrifice of the Magi's gifts. As God gives us the opportunity, let us make every minute of today's celebration resound with worship to the king who came to save his people.

Today, let us remember Jesus Christ—glorious God, perfect Son, eternal King. Let us draw near to the One who has drawn near to us. Let us come like the Magi, hear his word like Zechariah, believe his word like Mary, worship him like Elizabeth, and go tell of him like the shepherds.

For in the good news of his coming, we have found the greatest joy the world has ever known.

Scripture References
*— suggested daily reading

Genesis
3:1 - Day 3
4:2 - Day 19
12:2 - Day 12
15:4 - Day 2
16:1-16 - Day 2
17:4-7, 18:1 - Day 12
18:17-18 - Day 12
29:9 - Day 19
46:34 - Day 19
49:24 - Day 19

Exodus
3:1 - Day 19
30:1-10 - Day 2
30:11-16 - Day 16

Deuteronomy
18:15 - Day 23

1 Samuel
2:1-2 - Day 14
16:7 - Day 6
16:11 - Day 19

2 Samuel
7:1-17 - Day 5*
7:11b-12 & 16 - Day 17
22:3 - Day 14

1 Kings
19:11-12 - Day 4

Psalms
2:1-12 - Day 23
18:2 - Day 14
18:30 - Day 14
18:50 - Day 14
24 - Day 20*
87:5-6 - Day 16
103:1, 8 - Day 11
115:1 - Day 20
139:13 - Day 10

Isaiah
7:10-17 - Day 8*
8:5-17 - Day 8*
9:5 - Day 21
41 - Day 12*
53 - Day 18*
55:8 - Day 13

Jeremiah
31:33 - Day 23

Daniel
7:14 - Day 5
9:23 - Day 3

Micah
4:6-5:5 - Day 1*
5:2 - Day 17

Zechariah
13:1 - Day 23

Malachi
4:5-6 - Day 15

Matthew
1:18-25 - Day 7*, Day 8
2 - Day 23*
11:11 - Day 15
28:16-20 - Day 15*

Mark
10:35 - Day 16

Luke
1:1-4 - Day 3
1:5-25 - Day 2*, 3
1:16-17 - Day 15
1:20 - Day 6
1:24-25 - Day 10
1:26-33 - Day 4*
1:27 - Day 17
1:34-38 - Day 6*

1:38 - Day 8, 12
1:39-45 - Day 9*
1:45 - Day 6, Day 10
1:43 - Day 10
1:46-56 - Day 11*
1:57-66 - Day 13*
1:64 - Day 14
1:67-80 - Day 14*
1:76-79 - Day 15
2:1-7 - Day 16*, 18
2:4-5 - Day 17
2:8-20 - Day 22
2:8-14 - Day 19*
2:14 - Day 20
2:15-20 - Day 21*
3:21-22 - Day 20
6:22-23 - Day 9
6:45 - Day 6
9:28-36 - Day 20
10:1-20 - Day 22*
10:5 & 9 - Day 22
10:20 - Day 16
10:21 - Day 20
11:27-28 - Day 10
19:1-10 - Day 10*
19:11-27 - Day 24
20:19-26 - Day 16
23:47 - Day 20
24:51-31 - Day 24

John

1:12 - Day 4
1:14 - Day 20
1:46 - Day 4
3:1-21 - Day 25*
10:14 - Day 19
14:5 - Day 13
19:30 - Day 24
19:39 - Day 25
20:27-31 - Day 21

Acts

1:6-11 - Day 24*
4:12 - Day 5

Romans

3:24 - Day 7
3:26 - Day 7
5:8 - Day 18
15:20-21 - Day 22

1 Corinthians

6:19 - Day 9
15:47-48 - Day 6

Ephesians

1:3-10 - Day 16
1:5-6 - Day 4
2:1-2, 4-5, & 10 - Day 14
2:6-7 - Day 4

Philippians

2:1-11 - Day 17*

Colossians

1:19 - Day 5

1 Peter

2:4-10 - Day 8

1 John

1:1-3 - Day 21

Revelation

7:17 - Day 19
21:27 - Day 16
21:1-22:5 - Day 24

— Acknowledgements —

Truly, the foremost individual who has impacted me most in writing this book is Jesus Christ himself. Through my time in study, I have been increasingly astounded by the hope of his advent, the truth of his gospel, and the love of his salvation.

Many kind and talented individuals have been effective vessels of his hope, truth, and love. I will fail to remember all of them, but I want to take time to thank a few.

To Bethany, my wife, for always spurring me on to write and sing for the sake of the gospel. Your countless expressions of love, encouragement, and friendship have carried me for many years.

To Bryan, my fellow pastor and close friend, for taking the time to read these in their earliest form and helped push them to be more biblical, Christ-centered, and missional, just as you have done for me over the course of my life—and to Joy, who spent precious time editing this manuscript to help create this second edition.

To my church family at The Fields, for being my spiritual home and support through regular discipleship. My great joy is to get to walk in faith together every week to glorify Christ among the nations.

To my dad and mother-in-law, for kindly giving your time and talents to edit this book, and to my whole family, for your constant, loving support.

To my dear friends: Preston, for beginning this journey with me years ago, in pursuit of an honest and artful expression of this amazing story; Paul, for continuing to support my musical endeavors through your friendship and artistry; Grace, for your many hours of hard work to create this wonderful collection of art and bring this incredible story to life; the Moore family, for generously providing a wonderful retreat space where I was able to write the vast majority of this book; and many others who have listened, read, and supported me over the years.

To Andrew Peterson and The Rabbit Room, for inspiring this book and project with the incomparable *Behold The Lamb of God* and fostering the expansion of truly wonderful Christian art and community.

To everyone who backed this project on Kickstarter, for enabling all aspects of *Good News, Great Joy* to be recorded, printed, and shared. I could not have done this without you.

Thank you all.